Modern Ideas:
International Law and Freemasonry

Published by
P3rtınənt Press
an imprint of
Oxford Legal Publishing Limited
www.thepertinentpress.co.uk
OXFORD

"Publishers of Intelligent Books" © 2017

P3RTINƏNT PRESS
focuses on and aims to further study and knowledge in
philosophy, history, cultural studies, and theology.

P3rtınənt Press
is a registered trademark

Published in the United Kingdom by Oxford Legal Publishing Limited

Picture on the cover *Höhen und Tiefen der Erde in Lambert's Zenithal Projection von Hermann Berghaus*, 1878

First published 2020 by Oxford Legal Publishing Limited

British Library Cataloguing in Publication Data
Data Available

Oxford Legal Publishing Limited
is registered in England as No. 10898419
at the following address:
52 Cornmarket Street
Oxford OX1 3HJ

Pertinent Press is a translation work experience partner of the MA in Translation at

Goldsmiths
UNIVERSITY OF LONDON

ISBN: 978-1-912142-34-7

Ernest Nys

MODERN IDEAS
INTERNATIONAL LAW AND FREEMASONRY

Preface by Randall Lesaffer

Translated by Laura Stutt

P3rtınənt Press
OXFORD

Ernest Nys
(1851-1920)

TABLE OF CONTENTS

Preface

Randall Lesaffer

Professor of Legal History at KU Leuven, Belgium and Tilburg University, the Netherlands

AMONG THE LEADING INTERNATIONAL LAWYERS FROM AROUND the turn of the 20th century, the Belgian Ernest Nys (1851-1920) ranks as the field's foremost historian.[1] Although the historical work of Nys was by far the most extensive, profound and best researched, he completely underwrote the agenda of using history to celebrate modern international law as a vector of modernity, of peace, justice, humanity and civilisation among the nations of the world. His many contributions to the historiography stand out for their author's deep knowledge of historic scholarship and doctrinal developments of international as well as general legal and institutional history, reaching back to the rediscovery of Roman law in the 11th century. Nevertheless, his general historical outlook and programme was as teleological as that of those international lawyers for whom writing about its history was a more ancillary undertaking.

Ernest Nys shared the beliefs that underpinned modern international law's emergence as an autonomous and established academic discipline during the second half of the 19th century and that carried its rise as a significant discourse of international policies since. This belief system rested on three

1 Martti Koskenniemi, 'A history of international law histories', in Bardo Fassbender and Anne Peters (eds.), *The Oxford Handbook of the History of International Law* (Oxford University Press 2012) 943-71, at 943-4.

central pillars. Firstly, it considered the modern sovereign nation-state as foundational to the progress of international peace and justice. Whereas the ancient division of humanity into nations and states had brought anarchy and war, the modern form of the state would, with the aid of the managerial and organising role of international law, overcome this. Secondly, as the provenance of the sovereign nation-state and of international law were European, the progress of the old world would prove the progress of universal humankind through the spreading of the European system to other parts of the world. Thirdly, the role of the learned international law, and of the field's historian, was crucial in moulding international law into a complete, coherent and internally consistent scientific system of a quality similar to that of – codified – domestic law. Its historiography should thus focus on the study of its legal-technical doctrines and conceptions and of those learned writers who had most contributed to their elaboration.

Among the numerous studies on the history of international which Nys penned, his *Idées modernes, droit international et franc-maçonnerie* (1908),[2] takes a peculiar place. The booklet reads rather as a pamphlet which states and argues the role of Freemasonry in the development of international law than as a profound historical study in its author's familiar style. Nevertheless, the work is interesting as it forms one of the more express statements of the ideological views and agenda, with regard to international law but also to international and national politics at large.

---

2 Published Brussels: Weissebruch 1908. The booklet also appeared in a series of three articles in *Revue de droit international et de législation,* the first journal of international to which Nys contributed dozens of historical papers; see vol. 9 (1907) 717-41 and 10 (1908) 51-77 and 138-63.

The essayist and bold programmatic style of the text is reminiscent of the major historical work of Nys' most important teacher, François Laurent (1810-1887). The Ghent law professor Laurent, who is today mostly remembered as Belgium's foremost civil lawyer from the 19th century, penned between 1850 and 1870, an 18-volume long 'history' of international relations and law against the backdrop of his liberal, progressive and often idiosyncratic readings of human history and political philosophy.[3] The work is an excessively lengthy statement of the basic tenets of 19th-century political liberalism as applied to the international domain. Whereas it credits the role of classical Antiquity and Christianity in the slow maturation of humanity and civilisation in Europe, it is the modern nation-state which, after the French Revolution, brought about the conditions which made the real progress of the 19th century towards a common humanity, peace and justice, imaginable. These are popular sovereignty – the slaying of absolutism – and the separation of church and state – the slaying of religious oppression and intolerance.

The sovereignty of the people, secularisation and the equality among nations are what bind modernity, international law and Freemasonry together. To Nys, Freemasonry had, in the two centuries of its existence, acted as a significant mover behind the forces of history. It had been a nucleus of resistance against royal absolutism and church oppression, the promotor of the civil religion of Deism and tolerance and a prime force behind the revolutions of 1789 and beyond. Nys insisted

---

3 The four first volumes appeared under the title *Histoire du droit des gens et des relations internationales* (Ghent: L. Hebbelynck and J.-B Merry 1850); from volume 5 onwards *Etudes sur l'histoire de l'humanité* became the lead title but the older one still appeared as well (2nd edn., Ghent: Méline, Cans et Compagnie 1855-1870).

that leading international lawyers such as the Swiss Johann Kaspar Bluntschli (1808-1881) and Gustav Rolin-Jacquemyns (1835-1902), co-founder of the *Journal de droit international et de legislation comparée* (1868) and of the Institute of International Law (1873), were Freemasons.[4]

In the context of a panegyric on Freemasonry, the author's insistence on the role of secularisation, understood as the separation of church and state and religious tolerance, does not come as a surprise. This insistence also flowed from the context of Belgian politics and the personal biography of Nys. In the first half a century and more of the young state, which had gained its independence in 1830-1831, the clash between Catholics and liberals over the role of the Catholic Church in politics and society, and particularly in education, was a central fault line. Nys himself had become active in Ghent liberal circles while the *Université Libre de Bruxelles,* where he became a law professor in 1885, was a bulwark of anti-Catholic laicity and Freemasonry.

This English translation of international law of *Idées modernes, droit international et franc-maçonnerie* by Laura Stutt brings a text largely forgotten back into international circulation. Regardless of its specific subject, it gives a clear insight into the ideological agenda and sensitivities of the foremost framer of modern international law's historiography.

---

4 Frederik Dhondt, 'L'histoire, parole vivante du droit ? François Laurent en Ernest Nys als historiografen van het volkenrecht' in Bruno Debaenst (ed.), *De Belle Époque van het Belgisch Recht* (Brugge: Die Keure 2016) 91-115; Martti Koskenniemi, *The Gentle Civilizer of Nations. The Rise and Fall of Internationa Law 1870-1960* (Cambridge University Press 2002) 11-97.

ERNEST NYS (1851–1920), a Belgian lawyer and celebrated scholar, obtained his doctorate in law in 1874 at the University of Ghent, going on to study in Germany under the tuition of Bluntschli and Heffter. In 1876, he returned to Belgium and was admitted to the bar in Antwerp in 1877, becoming head of office at the Ministry of Justice in 1878. He entered the judiciary as a judge at the Court of First Instance at Antwerp and was later appointed judge at the Brussels Court of First Instance, becoming Vice President of the court on 6th December 1898, and finally a counsellor at the Brussels Court of Appeal on 10th September 1903. He was made President of Chamber at this court on 11th February 1920, only months before his death. Alongside his duties as a magistrate, he pursued a professional career at the Université Libre de Bruxelles between 1885 and 1920, holding numerous positions of note, including President of the Law Faculty (1898-1900). His interest in international law began to bear fruit with his first publication in 1879: *The Papacy Considered in Relation to International Law*. He had a strong connection to England, spending much time in the library at the British Museum. He translated James Lorimer's *Principles of International Law* (1885) and John Westlake's *Studies in International Law* (1895) into French, both fundamental works, and he was awarded honorary doctorates from the universities at Edinburgh, Glasgow and Oxford. The history of international law was a major theme in his works, but the breadth of his research is remarkable. He wrote on the political theories in England during the Middle Ages, the law of nations in relations between the Arabs and Byzantines, Honoré Bonet and Christine de Pisan, the primitive institutions of the High North, the utopians of the sixteenth century, and black slavery, to name but a few. Another recurring theme in his work was the historical relationship between the Papacy and the Masonic movement, to which *Modern Ideas: International Law and Freemasonry* is dedicated. His discourse could be scathing of any undemocratic behaviour, and he was generous in his criticism of tyrannical regimes. Paul Errera, speaking of Nys, wrote the following lines: "The extreme modesty of his life, which never knew worldly vanities, allowed only a few friends to approach him and fully appreciate him as a man... his heart was equal to his intelligence, which is no small thing to be said of him."

LAURA STUTT, a freelance translator, graduated with a Distinction in her Master's in Translation at Goldsmiths, University of London, in January 2020. She has a long-standing passion for language in all its forms. Before exploring translation, Laura studied Modern Languages and Linguistics at Newcastle University. She then completed a CELTA course at International House London and worked as a Business English teacher in Bogotá and an EFL teacher in London. Since concluding her studies in September 2019, Laura has translated Spanish and French texts into English in a range of domains, including medicine, journalism, law, and international politics. Laura currently resides in London with her Alaskan Malamute, Zelda, and and is pursuing a career in publishing as an editor.

Modern Ideas:
International Law and Freemasonry

Published by
P3rtınənt Press
an imprint of
Oxford Legal Publishing Limited
www.thepertinentpress.co.uk
OXFORD

"Publishers of Intelligent Books" © 2017

P3RTINƏNT PRESS
focuses on and aims to further study and knowledge in
philosophy, history, cultural studies, and theology.

P3rtınənt Press
is a registered trademark

Published in the United Kingdom by Oxford Legal Publishing Limited

Picture on the cover *Höhen und Tiefen der Erde in Lambert's Zenithal Projection von Hermann Berghaus*, 1878

First published 2020 by Oxford Legal Publishing Limited

British Library Cataloguing in Publication Data
Data Available

Oxford Legal Publishing Limited
is registered in England as No. 10898419
at the following address:
52 Cornmarket Street
Oxford OX1 3HJ

Pertinent Press is a translation work experience partner of the MA in Translation at

Goldsmiths
UNIVERSITY OF LONDON

ISBN: 978-1-912142-34-7

Ernest Nys

MODERN IDEAS
INTERNATIONAL LAW AND FREEMASONRY

Preface by Randall Lesaffer

Translated by Laura Stutt

P3rtınənt Press
OXFORD

Ernest Nys
(1851-1920)

TABLE OF CONTENTS

Preface

Randall Lesaffer

Professor of Legal History at KU Leuven, Belgium and Tilburg University, the Netherlands

AMONG THE LEADING INTERNATIONAL LAWYERS FROM AROUND the turn of the 20th century, the Belgian Ernest Nys (1851-1920) ranks as the field's foremost historian.[1] Although the historical work of Nys was by far the most extensive, profound and best researched, he completely underwrote the agenda of using history to celebrate modern international law as a vector of modernity, of peace, justice, humanity and civilisation among the nations of the world. His many contributions to the historiography stand out for their author's deep knowledge of historic scholarship and doctrinal developments of international as well as general legal and institutional history, reaching back to the rediscovery of Roman law in the 11th century. Nevertheless, his general historical outlook and programme was as teleological as that of those international lawyers for whom writing about its history was a more ancillary undertaking.

Ernest Nys shared the beliefs that underpinned modern international law's emergence as an autonomous and established academic discipline during the second half of the 19th century and that carried its rise as a significant discourse of international policies since. This belief system rested on three

---

1 Martti Koskenniemi, 'A history of international law histories', in Bardo Fassbender and Anne Peters (eds.), *The Oxford Handbook of the History of International Law* (Oxford University Press 2012) 943-71, at 943-4.

central pillars. Firstly, it considered the modern sovereign nation-state as foundational to the progress of international peace and justice. Whereas the ancient division of humanity into nations and states had brought anarchy and war, the modern form of the state would, with the aid of the managerial and organising role of international law, overcome this. Secondly, as the provenance of the sovereign nation-state and of international law were European, the progress of the old world would prove the progress of universal humankind through the spreading of the European system to other parts of the world. Thirdly, the role of the learned international law, and of the field's historian, was crucial in moulding international law into a complete, coherent and internally consistent scientific system of a quality similar to that of – codified – domestic law. Its historiography should thus focus on the study of its legal-technical doctrines and conceptions and of those learned writers who had most contributed to their elaboration.

Among the numerous studies on the history of international which Nys penned, his *Idées modernes, droit international et franc-maçonnerie* (1908),[2] takes a peculiar place. The booklet reads rather as a pamphlet which states and argues the role of Freemasonry in the development of international law than as a profound historical study in its author's familiar style. Nevertheless, the work is interesting as it forms one of the more express statements of the ideological views and agenda, with regard to international law but also to international and national politics at large.

---

2 Published Brussels: Weissebruch 1908. The booklet also appeared in a series of three articles in *Revue de droit international et de législation,* the first journal of international to which Nys contributed dozens of historical papers; see vol. 9 (1907) 717-41 and 10 (1908) 51-77 and 138-63.

The essayist and bold programmatic style of the text is reminiscent of the major historical work of Nys' most important teacher, François Laurent (1810-1887). The Ghent law professor Laurent, who is today mostly remembered as Belgium's foremost civil lawyer from the 19th century, penned between 1850 and 1870, an 18-volume long 'history' of international relations and law against the backdrop of his liberal, progressive and often idiosyncratic readings of human history and political philosophy.[3] The work is an excessively lengthy statement of the basic tenets of 19th-century political liberalism as applied to the international domain. Whereas it credits the role of classical Antiquity and Christianity in the slow maturation of humanity and civilisation in Europe, it is the modern nation-state which, after the French Revolution, brought about the conditions which made the real progress of the 19th century towards a common humanity, peace and justice, imaginable. These are popular sovereignty – the slaying of absolutism – and the separation of church and state – the slaying of religious oppression and intolerance.

The sovereignty of the people, secularisation and the equality among nations are what bind modernity, international law and Freemasonry together. To Nys, Freemasonry had, in the two centuries of its existence, acted as a significant mover behind the forces of history. It had been a nucleus of resistance against royal absolutism and church oppression, the promotor of the civil religion of Deism and tolerance and a prime force behind the revolutions of 1789 and beyond. Nys insisted

---

3 The four first volumes appeared under the title *Histoire du droit des gens et des relations internationales* (Ghent: L. Hebbelynck and J.-B Merry 1850); from volume 5 onwards *Etudes sur l'histoire de l'humanité* became the lead title but the older one still appeared as well (2nd edn., Ghent: Méline, Cans et Compagnie 1855-1870).

that leading international lawyers such as the Swiss Johann Kaspar Bluntschli (1808-1881) and Gustav Rolin-Jacquemyns (1835-1902), co-founder of the *Journal de droit international et de legislation comparée* (1868) and of the Institute of International Law (1873), were Freemasons.[4]

In the context of a panegyric on Freemasonry, the author's insistence on the role of secularisation, understood as the separation of church and state and religious tolerance, does not come as a surprise. This insistence also flowed from the context of Belgian politics and the personal biography of Nys. In the first half a century and more of the young state, which had gained its independence in 1830-1831, the clash between Catholics and liberals over the role of the Catholic Church in politics and society, and particularly in education, was a central fault line. Nys himself had become active in Ghent liberal circles while the *Université Libre de Bruxelles,* where he became a law professor in 1885, was a bulwark of anti-Catholic laicity and Freemasonry.

This English translation of international law of *Idées modernes, droit international et franc-maçonnerie* by Laura Stutt brings a text largely forgotten back into international circulation. Regardless of its specific subject, it gives a clear insight into the ideological agenda and sensitivities of the foremost framer of modern international law's historiography.

---

4 Frederik Dhondt, 'L'histoire, parole vivante du droit ? François Laurent en Ernest Nys als historiografen van het volkenrecht' in Bruno Debaenst (ed.), *De Belle Époque van het Belgisch Recht* (Brugge: Die Keure 2016) 91-115; Martti Koskenniemi, *The Gentle Civilizer of Nations. The Rise and Fall of Internationa Law 1870-1960* (Cambridge University Press 2002) 11-97.

Ernest Nys

Modern Ideas: International Law and Freemasonry

History demonstrates that particular events had a powerful influence on the development of international law, and certain nations provided the vital conditions for its application and reign.

With a system of legal regulations governing the relationships between political communities, the peoples' rights could only be enforced when these communities began to organise themselves in accordance with principles of justice, freedom and tolerance. By its very nature, such a system was incompatible with political despotism and religious fanaticism. Did despotism and fanaticism not prevent the State from fulfilling its international obligations? Could a sovereign who imagined himself divinely appointed treat with equality the peoples whose central institutions were based on the denial of his proud claims? Could a government which relied on a determined cult and which imagined itself to possess absolute truth live in peace with heretical or faithless nations?

Furthermore, cosmopolitanism and universalism were instrumental in shaping the rights of these peoples. Though these ideas certainly allowed for the concept of 'the homeland', they required that the formation of an enlarged homeland take precedence as the ultimate goal, destined to embrace all nations of a world that the cruel evils of war would desolate no longer.

Through affirmation of the maxims of equality before the law and of freedom of opinion and worship, through an effort to break the State's isolation and form the closest possible accord with other States, through a love of peace, and through an ardent desire to diminish the miseries of war, this goal would be achieved.

The venture was arduous; the struggle was fierce. A difficult task arose; absolutism must be toppled, and all modern liberties must be inscribed into charters and manifest as law. It was necessary to destroy the power that had always been assumed by the Churches, power that was used to persecute and inflict suffering.

Many eloquent writers have recounted the story of this centuries-long war, the battlefield spreading over entire continents. There is, however, a subject which most of them neglect to examine: the contribution from secret societies to the development of modern civilisation, and particularly that of Freemasonry.

At every period in history, the role of secret societies has been important. Some lines written by Madame de Stael in her book *De l'Allemagne* make a note of this fact, and justify it thus: "It is said that political institutions, social relations and often even those within the family do not reach beyond the most superficial aspects of life. It is therefore natural that throughout time we have sought some intimate way to acknowledge and understand each other; all those with a certain depth of character believe themselves to be followers, and seek to distinguish themselves from others by some sure sign." Previously, in the Middle Ages, Condorcet said in the *Esquisse d'un tableau historique des progrès de l'esprit humain* [Sketch for a Historical Picture of the Progress of the Human Mind]: "We shall examine whether, in a time when philosophical proselytism was so dangerous, this was the starting point of the perpetual destiny of secret societies; to silently and safely spread amongst a few followers a small number of simple truths as preservative safeguards against the dominant prejudices."

In the vast majority of cases, secretive societies were formed for the fortification of liberty and for the fight against political and religious despotism. Seeing the ineffectiveness of isolated efforts, those animated by the spirit of progress dreamt of uniting, their strength of attack and their strength of resistance thereby growing greater. Under the cover of secrecy, they increased their power; they engaged more readily with delivering, intact, to generations to come, the doctrines and traditions that they themselves had received for safekeeping. Masonry deserves to be placed in the first order of secret societies. For the past two centuries, all over the world, members of the lodges have been found leading the valiant who fight for the triumph of political liberty, religious tolerance, and understanding between peoples. The workshops themselves, on more than one occasion, have become involved in the fight. Ultimately, by its most fundamental principles, Masonry is the adversary of error, abuse and prejudice. Nevertheless, there has been an almost complete silence on the subject among historians.

This silence has an explanation. The work of Freemasonry is generally secretive. Without a doubt, the results are there, but a layman would struggle to say where they came from. Moreover, those rare writers who are aware of the actions of Masonry, at certain times and in important events, have not always shown real appreciation nor made an accurate assessment of the facts.

This is not the place to write a complete account of all of the lodges' activity. Here, we wish only to draw attention to certain key aspects.

One can broadly outline the mission accomplished by Freemasonry. More than any other institution, it has contributed to imparting importance and strength to public opinion and investing in it a degree of control; Freemasonry has worked to make the rights of civil power recognised, to reject the claims of the Churches, to impose tolerance in religious matters and to assert the secular character of the State. It has fought constantly to eliminate the religious element, the successor of the element of magic that prevailed in primitive societies, from all rules of law and from all legal demonstrations. As far as private law is concerned, it has never ceased to push for the useful legislative reforms brought about by the triumph of one of its fundamental principles: the principle of equality. In public law, more specifically, it has been the ruthless adversary of absolutism and has favoured with all its might the establishment and strengthening of the parliamentary system. Concerning the international sphere, where the cosmopolitan tendencies of Freemasonry quite naturally found application, it performed incalculable services; rising above the level of homelands, it could not avoid conquering the self-centred politics that would make foreign peoples into natural enemies; it preached universal alliance; it was the adversary of war and, even acting directly through military lodges, it was able, when war broke out, to attenuate evils and alleviate suffering.

One primary mode of action was the study and discussion of political issues within the lodges, often many years before they were subjected to public opinion. Masonry did not dictate dogma to its affiliates; it contented itself with formulating an ideal which members would strive to achieve; in short: Fraternity, liberty, equality, tolerance, and charity. This philosophical doctrine was broad enough to satisfy all men of good will. Moreover, Masonry offered the support which naturally resulted from such a collective effort; undoubtedly, the adversaries were powerful, but the followers were assured of effective protection. Masonry was relentlessly opposed; when, in some countries, the society was hatefully persecuted in attempts to extinguish its control, it never backed down. It well knew its own strength; in its rituals there were no complaints or whimpers. Masonry considered the enemy calmly; requesting neither favour nor grace, but promising justice in return for loyalty. "Let the unbelievers cease to be unjust to us," describes one instruction, "that they may seek the light and be treated with generosity."

CHAPTER I

THE ORIGINS OF FREEMASONRY. THE LEGENDS. THE FACTS

I

As we shall later ascertain, modern Masonry in fact dates from the beginning of the 18th century; however, it is worth reviewing some of the most prevalent theories that have been proposed about its origins, and briefly recall the history of other organisations that, like Masonry, were dedicated to fighting for the liberation of the human spirit, and which, again like Masonry, enveloped themselves in mystery and secrecy.

We know the prevailing legends. One traces the institution back to Solomon gifting the architect Hiram, son of a Tyrian and a Naphtali tribeswoman, with the stewardship and the management of the construction of a temple to be erected in Jerusalem. The workers, numbering 183,000, were divided into three classes that had various words, signs and touches to recognise each other and to receive remuneration proportionate to their specific work. Another legend describes Masonry as the heir of the colleges of sages and priests of Chaldee, India and Egypt, who imparted moral and scientific doctrines and submitted their disciples to initiation ordeals. Let us not forget, though, that such antiquated and esoteric mysteries had just cause to be so. One illustrious scholar indicated how each phase is marked by its relationship with science: at the commencement of civilisation, all knowledge assumed a religious and mystical form; this was followed by a period half-rationalist and half-mystical, and at last, there came pure science. A third legend pertains to the Order of the Knights Templar; it details how Jacques de Molay, the last Grand Master of the Order of the Temple, some time before he burned on the pyre, made four inscriptions at the back of his dungeon in which he entrusted the task of avenging his memory.

One ostensibly scientific theory links Freemasonry to the stone masons' guilds that once occupied Germany. There are various facts and dates to support this: in 1459, the German stonemasons' guilds met in Regensburg as a general guild; at the end of the 15th century they formed a league headed by the four lodges of Strasbourg, Cologne, Zurich and Vienna. The *Bauhutte* was a barrack, a provisional building that housed the workers. The Latin base-word was *loggia*; the word *lodge* being English, and *loge* French.

The true historical background differs. Freemasonry has its roots in England and Scotland, and its formation has a simple explanation. It arose from the introduction of members who were active in trade into the companies or guilds of stonemasons. To use the usual terms of the French rituals, it was born when Masons of theory met Masons of trade; the Masons of theory who "taught morality and engaged only in liberal thought" were received into the lodges hitherto composed of "workers who erected buildings materially"; according to English writers, Freemasonry was born when *speculative* Masonry penetrated the workshops of *operative* Masonry.

In English, the words *free mason* have been in use since the middle of the 14th century; they perhaps served to designate the master stonemasons in their profession who, free of commitment binding them to their guild, could henceforth go wherever the great works called them. One particular expression appears in an act from the reign of Edward III, that of *mestre Mason de franche peer* [master Mason of free stone], meaning skilful master Mason; the terms *franche peer* and *free stone* (polished stone), were at variance with *grosse peer* [rough-rruson] and *rough stone*. When those not engaged in the trade were accepted into the guilds of stonemasons, they were designated by the term *accepted Masons*, that is to say elected Masons, while *admitted Masons* were those who entered the societies by virtue of an apprenticeship or their heritage.

A thoroughly competent writer, Count Goblet d'Alviella, teaches that modern Freemasonry emerged from the fraternities and not from the corporations themselves. "Alongside the organisation of trade," he writes, "or rather one aspect of said organisation, its charitable and mutualist side, was the fraternity (*fraternitas, Bruderschaft, broederscap, brotherhood* or *fellowship*). It was generally presided over by a Master, but both Companions and Masters were more or less on an equal footing." On the other hand, and it is important to take note of this, the fraternity could accept, at least as honorary members, foreigners into the profession. The charter granted in 1260 by the Bishop of Basel to the tailors of this city contains the following clause: "The same conditions are applicable to those who do not work in the trade and who wish to enter the fraternity."

According to our learned author, in several countries, notably in Germany, Belgium and France, the Masters eventually withdrew from these fraternities which, in the hands of the Companions, became societies of mutual resistance and aid; in the British Isles, it played out differently: Masters,

Companions and even Apprentices remained members of the fraternities, and it is in these fraternities rather than in the workshops themselves that the antecedents of speculative Masonry must be sought. Count Goblet d'Alviella cites the case of the *Worshipful Company of Masons* of the City of London. "The lodge at Masons Hall," he wrote, "or the *Acception* as it was called, was not synonymous with the company. The latter was composed of professionals only. The lodge, whose members bore the title of accepted Masons, like their ancestors at *Bruderschaften*, comprised both professionals and speculatives. Moreover, not all the members of the company were necessarily members of the *Acception*. We can trace the *Acception's* existence from 1620 to 1678. We therefore have the evocative idea of a lodge which not only admits speculatives alongside professionals, and grants the title of Companion to Master Masons of the trade, but which is still in the process of building itself alongside and apart from practical Masonry."

II

By the 17th century, non-professionals were already entering the lodges. While initially rare, little by little they grew in number, in most lodges eventually overtaking the professionals. Nevertheless, in a few lodges the workers continued to be preponderant; this was the case until 1842 for the *Saint John* lodge in Glasgow. The 'speculative' element prevented the abandonment of the practices and customs of the 'operative' organisation; there they collected legends, emblems, and symbols; they adhered to the rules; they took advantage of all elements of the mysterious and secret system: signs, passwords, touches. But the old occupations which mainly concerned executing construction works were replaced with new duties, a new task and a new mission; while aid and charity did not cease to be man's primordial obligations, the conquest of freedom, the realisation of political and social reforms, the affirmation of tolerance in religious matters, and the reign of peace were equally noble goals. "The brotherhood amidst real workers," said Findel, "became a brotherhood among symbolic workers; the work of the spirit came to replace the work of technical art, and instead of visible temples that could be erected and destroyed, it became a question of working to build the unique and invisible temple of the spirit."

Concerning the first manifestations of the movement that was to transform Freemasonry and make it a universal institution, there is accurate information dating back to the first years of the 17th century. According to documents from 1620 concerning the *Company of Masons of the City*, based in London, in this year there were already several non-professional members of the society who had meetings on its premises. One initiation in particular stands out as an important date; that of Sir Robert Murray, quartermaster general of the Scottish army, who was accepted in Newcastle, 20th May, 1641, by members of the Edinburgh lodge. Let us not forget that, twenty years later, Sir Robert Murray featured amongst the founders of the Royal Society of London, which itself began as a secret society.

In his autobiography, Elie Ashmole, the famous antiques dealer, discusses Freemasonry at various points. On 16th October, 1646, he writes that he was accepted as a Freemason at Warrington, at the same time as Colonel Mainwaring; in all likelihood this was a temporary lodge held at Warrington precisely for the purpose of initiating these two neophytes. Ashmole also names the members who were present at the ceremony; some were complete strangers to the stonemason profession; they were 'Masons of theory' not 'practising Masons'. On 11th March, 1682, he recalls that he attended a meeting held at the premises of the *Company of Masons of the City*, in which laymen were accepted as Freemasons.

In 1686, the curator of the Ashmole Museum in Oxford, Robert Plot, published his book: *The Natural History of Staffordshire*; he mentions the presence of Freemasons in the county of Stafford, and adds that Freemasons were widespread throughout England. "People of the highest birth," he said, "are not above becoming members of the society and it is even fashionable to be initiated."

In 1688, the *Academy of Armory* appeared. The author, Randle Holme, speaks of fraternities, societies or companies of people of the same profession united by oath; he writes that in these fraternities there are generally one or two masters and two supervisors; he reproduces the terms that designated and were used by "free masons stone cutters", and adds that he himself is part of a guild.

According to another writer, John Aubrey, Sir Christopher Wren, the illustrious architect, was accepted as a Mason during the great meeting of the "fraternity of the adopted Masons", which was held on 18th March, 1691, in the Church of St. Paul in London. This must be accurate. Upon the death of Sir Christopher Wren in 1723, newspapers noted that he had been "a worthy free mason".

The Scottish stonemasons' lodges claimed to be connected with the builders and builders' guilds which, in the 12th century, erected the abbeys of Kelso, Melrose and Kilwinning. The lodges of Melrose and Kilwinning even debate over who came first. Without a doubt, their significant antiquity is well substantiated; while the *Lodge Mother Kilwinning* holds documents that predate 1642, the *Lodge of Melrose* can cite minutes dating back to 1674 that contain proof that it existed before that year. The *Lodge Kelso* possesses archives dating back to 1701. For its part, the *Mary's Chapel* lodge in Edinburgh holds ancient records of minutes dating back to 1599. One lodge in Glasgow dates back to 1628. The old lodge at Dundee is from the same year. On the register of the Brechir lodge of 1723 there is a copy of the regulations of 1714.

These were professional Masons' societies, 'operative' lodges; these lodges had, moreover, a useful role: their supervisors, the 'wardens', handled the members of the magistrates of the district and exercised control.

It has been proven that in 1600 a non-professional, John Boiswell, was accepted to the *Ancient Lodge of Edinburgh*; other initiations of non-professionals took place in the same lodge in 1634, 1633, 1637 and 1642. In 1670, of the forty-nine members of the Aberdeen Lodge, thirty-nine were complete strangers to the art of construction.

At the end of the 17th century and at the beginning of the 18th century, there were, both in England and Scotland, a certain number of Masonic lodges where professionals and non-professionals were admitted. One can substantiate this claim with the testimony of an enemy of the Masonic order, Samuel Prichard, who, in 1730, published a brochure in London titled: 'Masonry dissected', with the aim of attacking the lodges.

> But in these latter Days Masonry is not composed of Artificers, as it was in its primæval State, when some few Catechetical Questions were necessary to declare a Man sufficiently qualified for an Operative Mason. The Terms of

> Free and Accepted Masonry (as it now is) has not been heard of till within these few Years.

He even quoted a date following which nobles, lawyers and merchants were initiated in great numbers: 1691. According to James Anderson, writing with full knowledge of the facts, London alone housed seven lodges in the last decade of the 17th century.

"In recent times," he wrote, "Masonry has ceased to be composed of workers as it once was, when it was necessary to be a stonemason. Until a few years ago, the terms Free and Accepted Masons were not heard of."

At that time, the lodges did not recognise a higher authority; they had no allegiance to any central institution; they were formed by the free will of Freemasons who had no need of letters of constitution to install a workshop. However, they had the same signs, the same passwords; they had their charters, their 'Constitutions', which proclaimed in almost identical terms the same fundamental maxims.

III

In 1717, something occurred in London that produced the most fortunate consequences for the future of the Masonic institution. On 24th June of that year, four lodges, according to some, or six lodges according to others, held an assembly in which they formed a Grand Lodge and elected a Grand Master. One of these lodges appears to have been composed of non-professionals, and in the others, professionals and non-professionals rubbed shoulders together. The original idea was to establish close links between the existing workshops in the

City of London and the City of Westminster, but soon the new organisation exerted influence over a number of provincial lodges; it created new workshops, and extended its activity over Ireland, Scotland, and other European countries, stretching to the continents of America, Africa and Asia.

The first Grand Master was Anthony Sayer, an important official in finance administration. Sayer retired on 24th June 1718 and was replaced by George Payne, to whom Jean-Theophile Desaguiliers succeeded in 1719. Payne again occupied the presidency in 1720; then in 1721, the Duke of Montagu replaced him, commencing a series of nobles and princes of royal blood who, thereafter, were raised to Grand Mastery and steered English Masonry towards its destiny.

On 29th September 1721, the Grand Lodge commissioned James Anderson to redraft the old Constitutions. Each lodge possessed, under the name of Constitutions, a true charter, in which were written, as we shall come to see, the fundamental maxims. There were a number of manuscripts, some of which dated back rather far. On 27th December, the Grand Master Duke of Montagu had Anderson's work submitted to fourteen brothers, and, on 23rd March 1722, they produced a favourable assessment while proposing slight corrections. On 17th January 1723, the work was presented to the Grand Lodge, which ordered its publication. The book was published in 1723, under the title: *The Constitutions of the free-masons, containing the history, charges, regulations, etc., of that most ancient and right worshipful fraternity. For the use of the lodges.*

Heading the volume, which comprised 92 quarto pages, was a dedication signed by Desaguiliers, succeeded by a historical overview of Freemasonry, the "charges", that is to say the duties of the Freemason, the general rules, and finally songs and poetry. The historical overview and the part of the book concerning the duties of the Freemason were the work of Anderson; the general rules had been compiled by George Payne and two other dignitaries.

Anderson has been criticised for embellishing the ancient legends; for not having written a true history of the Masonic institution. It should be noted, however, that he included an interesting account of events that had occurred since 1717 in the new edition he published in 1738 under the title: *The new book of Constitutions of the most ancient and honourable fraternity of free and accepted Masons.* Regardless, he endeavoured to recall, in his account of the origins, how the art of construction was an honour of the highest antiquity in Egypt, in Asia Minor, among the Greeks and Romans, and how it was encouraged in England and Scotland. He recounted the legend detailing how Prince Edwin, son of the Saxon king Athelstan, summoned, around the year 930, all the Masons of the kingdom to meet in York and held a Grand Lodge in the city. Anderson described the kings of England and Scotland encouraging the "royal art" and mentioned James I, Charles I and Charles II, adding that under James II's reign the lodges of London "fell into ignorance" but after the revolution of 1688, King William favoured the beneficent institution. According to Anderson, there is reason to believe that Charles II was a Freemason as well as William III.

The section of the book dealing with the duties of the Freemason and titled: 'The charges of a free-mason' consisted almost entirely of the reproduction of the old constitutions of guilds and stonemasons' societies; these documents dated far back, some even to the year 1600. But on one important point, changes were introduced.

With regard to the duties of the Freemason concerning God and religion, the ancient texts said that he must be faithful to God and the holy Church, and not fall into error or heresy. The new doctrine was broader. "A *Mason*," he writes, "is oblig'd by his Tenure to obey the moral Law; and if he rightly understands the Art, he will never be a stupid *Atheist* nor an irreligious *Libertine*. But though in ancient Times Masons were charg'd in every Country to be of the Religion of that Country or Nation, whatever it was, yet 'tis now thought more expedient only to oblige them that Religion in which all Men agree, leaving their particular Opinions to themselves; that is, to be *good Men and true*, or Men of Honour and Honest, by whatever Denominations or Persuasions they may be distinguish'd; whereby Masonry becomes the *Center* of *Union*, and the Means of conciliating true Friendship among Persons that must else have remain'd at a perpetual Distance."

Undoubtedly, this proclamation underlined the necessity to believe in a Supreme Being, but it was also asserting that religion could no longer serve to divide and oppose men as irreconcilable enemies; it was at the same time far ahead of the legislation in force in all countries, and even in Great Britain where tolerance still did not apply to all denominations and opinions. We will later see from what philosophical source the precept adopted by the English Masonry of 1717 was derived; let us here be content to note the undeniable importance for the cause of progress; this association whose members spread throughout the globe, adopting as fundamental rules those proposed by James Anderson, according to which the claims of the churches to exclusive domination were finally in vain, and according to which goodness, sincerity and loyalty would constitute the supreme virtues. Moreover, let's hasten to add, the "deism" affirmed in 1717 was not intended to remain the immutable principle and for a long time a significant portion of Freemasonry maintained a more widespread tolerance than that which is limited to the worshippers of a God.

Following the duties of the Freemason towards God and religion, Anderson describes the duties "of the Civil Magistrate, supreme and subordinate". The English lodges were necessarily favourable to the royal family of Hanover, whose first representative, George I, ascended to the throne in 1716. For these lodges, in fact, the son of James II, the Knight of St. George, as he was called, embodied the general reaction in political and religious matters. Protégé of the court of France and court of Spain, was he not prepared to accept the support of the hereditary enemies of his homeland and invade Britain? "A *Mason,*" it is said in the 'duties', "is a peaceable Subject to the Civil Powers, wherever he resides or works. Thus he must be careful never to enter into plots or conspiracies contrary to the peace and prosperity of this nation nor to act as a disobedient man towards the lower magistrates; for as Masonry has always been outraged by war, murder and chaos, so the ancient kings and princes have been very keen to encourage the Mason workers because of their peacefulness and *Loyalty,* by which they have always eluded the evil intentions and quarrels of their adversaries, and have increased the honour of the brotherhood that has always flourished in times of peace. So that if a Brother should be a Rebel against the State, he is not to be tolerated in his Rebellion, however he may be pitied as an unhappy Man; and if convicted of no other Crime, though the loyal Brotherhood must and ought to disown his Rebellion, and give no Umbrage or Ground of political Jealousy to the Government for the time being; they cannot expel him from the *Lodge*, and his Relation to it remains indefeasible."

The development of Masonry and the proliferation of its principles were rapid, especially following the accession of the Duke of Montagu to the position of Grand Master.

Proof of this can be found in the "official lists" which, from 1724 until 1778, were executed by order of the Grand Lodge of England and where were registered, generally with the date of their creation, the lodges which depended on the Grand Lodge; there is further proof thanks to the minutes of the Grand Lodge of England, which begin on 25th November, 1723; here are listed, for many years, the regularly constituted lodges and there are even records of the names of venerable attendants, supervisors and members.

From a close examination of the documents, it follows that, from 1723, fifty-two lodges recognised the supremacy of the Grand Lodge of England; in 1730, the figure rose to one hundred and four and, in 1755, to two hundred and seventy-one. As we have seen, several workshops predated 1717; in 1721, three lodges were created; in 1724, four lodges were founded; the active proliferation did not cease. Soon, moreover, it extended to Ireland and Scotland. A Grand Lodge was established in Munster in 1726; but in 1730 it merged with the Grand Lodge which in that year had been established in Dublin; a Grand Lodge was inaugured in Edinburgh in 1736. In this same period, the Masonic conquest of the European continent, America, Africa and Asia began.

We will later have an opportunity to look over the dates, figures and facts more closely. For now, let us mention the guide provided by James Anderson himself in the edition of the Constitutions which appeared in 1738. When it came to the matter of creating a lodge in a remote country, the Grand Master would give a Mason letters by which he would confer upon him the power to act as his deputy; the document was called “the deputation”. The first “deputation” concerned Gibraltar; the second Madrid, both occurring prior to 1730; other “deputations” related to Bengal, Lower Saxony, the colony of New Jersey in America, Lisbon, on the borders of Gambia on the African coast, and at Cape Coast Castle also in Africa. Some deputations concerned special missions; such was the case for the authorisation given, in 1731, to Lord Chesterfield, ambassador for The Hague, to hold the lodge where the Duke of Lorraine was accepted.

James Anderson, whose work we have just summarised, was a man of merit. Born in Aberdeen around 1680, in 1710 he became minister of a Presbyterian church in London. It is thought that in his youth he was part of the Aberdeen lodge, which, as we have seen, already consisted, in 1670, of non-professionals. Desaguiliers signed the dedication of Constitutions, and if he was not precisely Anderson's collaborator, it is highly likely that he exerted some influence over him. Jean-Theophile Desaguiliers was born in France in 1683. He was the son of Jean des Aguiliers, who, as a protestant pastor near La Rochelle, had to take refuge with his family first in Guernsey and later England when, in 1685, Louis XIV revoked the Edict of Nantes. After studying at Oxford, he became chaplain of the Duke of Chandos. He was a member of the Royal Society and was held in high esteem by Isaac Newton. He died in 1744.

IV

One point is beyond doubt: the transformation of the lodges that took place at the end of the 17th century and the beginning of the 18th century was closely linked to the intellectual movement that took place around the same time in England. A Masonry historian notes: "The last, and at the same time most decisive agent in accomplishing the transformation of Masonry," writes Joseph Findel, "was that intellectual movement known under the name of English Deism, which boldly rejected all Revelation and all religious Dogmas, and under the victorious banner of reason and criticism, broke down all barriers in its path." In politics, the theory of divine law had succumbed to national law; the parliamentary system was firmly established. In science, the principles of inductive reasoning proclaimed by Francis Bacon, at the beginning of the 17th century, had definitively triumphed. A new assault was unleashed on the notion of authority. Courageous writers attacked the churches' attempts to control mankind's intellectual development, and demanded the right of reason.

English deism was essentially the doctrine of tolerance; in this respect, it exerted great influence on the members of the lodges who were among the leaders in the events we have just recalled. By modifying the text of *Duties of a Freemason*, by deleting any mention of the "Holy Church" and by no longer condemning heresy, the redactors of the *Constitutions* and *Charges* of 1723 only applied ideas defended so courageously by John Toland, Anthony Collins, and Matthew Tindal, to mention but these names.

Judging by one of his books published in 1720, John Toland was initiated to Masonry. In any event, in his *Pantheisticon* he described an association whose members adopted a softer and purer religion than religions based on authority, proclaimed freedom of thought and freedom of action while repelling licentiousness, and wandered as the sworn enemies of all tyrants, "whether they be despotic monarchs, proud nobles or even factious leaders of the crowd." It is a curious work; it does not seem that the author simply drew from his imagination and neither does it seem that he wanted to portray a secret society other than Freemasonry. *Pantheisticon* is written in Latin. According to the title, it is "the Form of Celebrating the Socratic Society... the Morals and Axioms of the Pantheists or the Brother-Hood"; by the word "pantheists", Toland refers to free thinkers. The book contains a description of society through instructions contained in the president and members' questions and answers to each other. It tells us the fundamental maxims: tolerance, love of freedom, and finally equality.

The liberal principle that the lodges preached to their followers with regard to the cults had been incompletely affirmed in the Toleration Act of 1689. William III was unsuccessful in getting the generous provision adopted which, in his mind, should extend to all sects and all beliefs; but, even incomplete, the law had a significant meaning. It proved, indeed, the will of the political society to exist outside any religious ideology. Furthermore, it produced useful results. At the testimony of Buckle, at the end of the 18th century, clerical influence diminished in England by considerable proportions; until then, many dignitaries of the Anglican Church had occupied high positions in the State. In 1713, for the last time in history, a bishop, Bristol's John Robinson, Lord Privy Seal, represented Great Britain in an international congress. Another historian, Lecky, notes that, around the same time, industrial interests and commercial spirit became preponderant at the expense of theological influence. In addition, the year 1717 saw the disappearance of one of the clergy's instruments of domination: by an act of force, the government prorogued the "convocation", the assembly representing the clergy. For a long time, it had been feared and had caused the most serious of difficulties; from then until 1850, every year, this same measure was taken.

The English Masonic lodges were a force to be reckoned with when it came to propagating the ideas of progress from the beginning of the 18th century. It should not be forgotten that they were recruiting from the influential classes of society: nobles, civil servants, officers of the land and sea forces, members of the liberal professions, merchants, and captains of ships were received in an association that soon offered the invaluable advantage of possessing branches all over the globe where the Mason brothers found friends and protectors. The lodges, moreover, made sure that only men of high calibre were admitted. According to an ancient textbook, given that morality and philanthropy formed the basis of the institution, every aspirant had to have received a liberal education and act honourably at all times; he had to be of irreproachable morals, of scrupulous loyalty, of a conciliatory and good character, and his discretion must be iron-clad. "In profane society, he will be free without licence, great without pride, humble without baseness; in Masonic society, he will be firm without being stubborn, severe without being inflexible, submissive without being servile. Always just and courageous, he will defend against oppression, protect innocence, and never calculate its benefits and services."

CHAPTER II

SECRET SOCIETIES WITH PHILOSOPHICAL, SCIENTIFIC OR LITERARY OBJECTIVES

I

THE MOVEMENT THAT TOOK PLACE IN THE LODGES OF GREAT Britain at the beginning of the 18th century was ever more beneficial in its effects, with Masonry seeing the ranks of its followers strengthened thanks to the affiliation of those who until then, in other associations for the most part cloaked in mystery, had fought for the emancipation of the human spirit.

In the first lines of this book, we spoke about the help furnished on civilisation by secret societies, which, at every period in history, have collaborated in grandiose work. Without going back further, we can mention the Italian academies of the 15th and 16th centuries, the literary and scientific sodalities constituted in Germany in the 17th century, and the associations formed in England in the 17th century. The members of these fraternities entered the Masonic temples as soon as they noticed that they were being offered, together with assistance, the certitude of proliferation.

A common feature of all these associations, whether their aim was scientific, literary, political or social, was their will to restore to man the dignity that prejudices had taken from him. For some, it was political independence in particular that had to be conquered; for others, the objective was to break the principle of authority in the scientific field and to lead the study of nature to triumph. All were animated by the new spirit, which the words freedom, tolerance and fraternity accurately described. For these associations, there were neither distinctions of rank nor differences of religion; for them, the fatherland did not impose narrow exclusivism; they were egalitarian and cosmopolitan in their vows and in their tendencies. They were also fighting the same enemies: despotism and the Churches.

A historian, Christian Bartholmess, described the Italian academies standing up to the universities. "He then who says School", he writes, "means the traditional exhibition of opinions consecrated by the centuries; he who says Academy, means to designate the independent quest for truth or the free contemplation of beauty." Almost all the academies had been presided over by the ecclesiastic authority; they had been forced to take refuge in mystery and to surround in secrecy their meetings and even the names of their members; many of them had adopted a ritual and symbols for their sessions, and we can see that, as in Freemasonry, the art of construction had provided the signs, emblems and terminology.

At that period, for people of the church, the word 'academy' awakened the idea of heresy; scientific societies were linked to the sects of the Middle Ages, especially to the Vaudois (the Waldensians); they were accused of being the descendants of Gnosticism or even of originating from Mahometism. The truth was that, in their own words, they were the enemies of all positive religion: their members were rebels who, like rebels of any period, had to break the existing social edifice before dreaming of building a city of justice and truth.

Even those who claimed to be confined to the realm of science were considered dangerous and reprehensible: Were they not contesting the alleged duty of obedience; were they not teaching that nature was "the source and rule of life"? Speaking of the members of the Cosenza Academy founded by Bernardin Telesio, Bartholmess describes them seeking the foundations of philosophy and poetry in the observation of nature. Telesio appealed to living, active knowledge. Thomas Campanella blamed "the souls attached to dead books and temples, unfaithful copies of the living book". Galilee said that philosophy is written in the great book of nature.

One ingenious writer endeavoured to gather information on some of these academies and secret societies. According to Louis Keller, it is a proven fact that almost all the leading minds of the 17th century belonged to secret societies, not only scholars like Bacon, Galilee, Boyle, Comenius, Leibniz, but a king, princes and men of state, such as Charles-Gustave of Sweden, the Great Elector Frederic-Guillaume, the Chancellor of Sweden Axel Oxenstierna, Oliver Cromwell and Christian d'Anhalt. "More than any state or church," he writes, "these academies and societies laid the foundation for the admirable movement of modern times; they have been the supporters of philosophical thought, they have made victorious the notion of tolerance."

Among these societies are almost all the academies that have been formed in Italy since the middle of the 15th century. A few mentions are enough. Pomponio Leto founded the *Academia Romana* in Rome, which met in the catacombs; Pope Paul II persecuted the association with extreme rigour; in 1468, twenty members were arrested on charges of paganism; Pomponio Leto was thrown into the dungeons of the Castel Sant'Angelo; Bartolommeo Platina was tortured. In Naples, Jean-Baptiste Porta created the *Accademia dei secreti*, which the Inquisition immediately decided to destroy. A remarkable physicist, Porta was accused of witchcraft. "His insatiable curiosity", says one writer, "strives to discover in all things that which is *curiosum, reconditum, novum, arcanum, occultum.* Creation, in his eyes, is an inexhaustible source of mysteries and wonders."

At that time, the words *magia naturalis*, "natural magic", designated the still unexplained part of physics, the advancement of physical sciences that many associations proposed. Already we have cited the *Academia cosentina* or *Telesiana*, destined to fight the tyranny of Aristotelian-ism, to teach a philosphy less burdened with obstacles and to propagate the new system in which reason and experience are combined. Some of these fraternities have branches; such is the case for the *Academia magna* in Florence. "There was hardly a city that did not have an academy", said Bartholmess, "the somewhat considerable cities had several."

Secret societies with literary or scientific tendencies are well established in Germany; some focus on the national language, for others the study of nature is the main goal; their work is wrapped in mystery, like the Italian fraternities with which they are associated. Louis d'Anhalt-Köthen was accepted, in 1600, as member of the *Accademia della Crusca* of Florence. Along with some friends, the prince created, in 1617, in Weimar, the *Société du Palmier* [Palm Tree Society], the *Palmbaum*, which, for thirty or forty years, remained a secret society and comprised, from 1617 to 1662, seven hundred and eighty-nine members, including a king, three electors, forty-seven dukes, sixty counts, nobles, scientists, and the bourgeoisie. Oxenstierna, Chancellor of Sweden, was a member of the Palmbaum, as well as, to quote the name of an important figure in the history of ideas, Jean-Valentin Andreæ. Also in 1617, Princess Anna, wife of Christian I, Prince of Anhalt-

Bernburg, founded the *Noble Académie des loyales*, a society to which only women were admitted. In 1619, Joachim Jungius founded *the Societas quoerentium* or *Collegium philosophicum* in Rostock, modelled on the Italian sodalites, for the study of natural sciences and for experimental research.

The *Deutsche Societät* [German Society] of Konigsberg dates back to 1631, which included among its members high-ranking officials, doctors, mathematicians, and musicians. The *Société des trois roses* [Society of Three Roses] of Hamburg dates back to 1653.

The aforementioned Protestant theologian, Jean-Valentin Andreæ, was the founder of secret society *Fraternitas christiana*. He was one of the noblest people of his time; he was animated by neighbourly love, and dreamed of uniting all men in evangelical doctrine; Via the "Christian fraternity", which he founded in 1620, he wanted to establish an indissoluble bond between the leaders of all countries. Several years later, another great spirit, Jean Amos Comenius, spoke to Andreæ with a view to forming a society that recruited members independently of their homeland. Tolerance and freedom were its fundamental maxims. The theologian then recalled the efforts that he had just made, the success that had initially crowned them, the obstacles that the frightening religious war had inflicted on Central Europe since 1618, and he entrusted the reformer with the arduous task of continuing the work.

London was at that time the headquarters of the spirit of progress and, to use a modern expression, the 'genius' of the revolution. Many refugees from the continent brought their plans, their dreams, their strong convictions; from the provinces of England there rushed all those who wanted, even by brutal force, to put an end to the incessant provocations of the monarchy; the capital, for its part, had enough men of value and will that all circumstances favoured the development of new ideas and the actualisation of important reform. Comenius dreamt of establishing the *Collegium Catholicum* in London, whose foundation he wished would comprise all academies and all societies, and which was to form as a superior organisation. However, political events impeded the realisation of his wishes and, in 1642, he went to Sweden.

One of Comenius' friends was altogether more fortunate; Samuel Hartlieb, born in Elbing, arrived in England around 1628, and created a curious situation there. Linked with many distinguished men, he was, as one of his biographers says, concerned with literary, scientific, theological and political "information"; he was thus like the general secretary of the whole intellectual movement. He was active from 1630 to 1650 and it seems certain that he formed, under the name of *Macaria*, a secret society intended to promote liberal ideas. Already, under the title *A description of the famous kingdom of Macaria*, he had sketched, in 1644, the plan of an ideal kingdom, modelled on Thomas More's *Utopia* and Francis Bacon's *New Atlantis*. It should not be forgotten, moreover, that at the same time the Invisible College was formed in London, into which Sir Robert Boyle entered in 1646 and which, a few years later, renounced the veil of mystery with which it had surrounded itself and became the glorious Royal Society.

II

THE ROSE CROSS MUST ALSO BE MENTIONED. IT SEEMS THAT THE word first appeared in 1603. "The name was allegorical", writes an author from the end of the 18th century. "The cross denoted the holiness of union; the rose was the image of discretion: the two words united mean a holy discretion.

According to some, it was simply a name given to those who dealt with occult sciences; according to others, it denoted an association whose members, numbering twelve, possessed mysterious knowledge and propagated doctrine according to which a divine soul or energy is spread throughout the universe; according to others yet, at the beginning of the 17th century, societies were formed in several countries following the publication of the writings of Jean-Valentin Andreæ, in which he endeavoured to prove that the research of alchemists, inspired by the love of gold, must expose them to criticism and blame. Here he also reproduced the legend according to which, in the first half of the 15th century, after long journeys to Asia, Africa, and Spain, Christian Rosenkreutz brought back the secrets of the Orient and created the Fraternity of the Rose Cross. It is difficult to admit that publications dedicated to an imaginary society led to the generation of fraternities that proposed an identical goal to that of that very society. Moreover, in chronological order, Andreæ's writings on "the renown of the association of the Rose Cross" and on "the Chymical Wedding of Christian Rosenkreutz" are posterior, it seems, to the use of the term Rose Cross.

Whether the Rose Cross remained an isolated few, or formed a single association, or constituted diverse societies in Germany, Italy, Switzerland, the United Provinces, and England, one fact is certain: they took considerable action. They claimed to be innovative thinkers; their teaching was linked to bold theories; often even official and orthodox science summarised its condemnations by calling the daring thinker who refused to bow down to its dogmas a Rose Cross. Here was the battle between dialectic and experience, the latter having to dethrone the former if one wanted progress to reign triumphant. Here too religious fanaticism and tolerance met in confrontation. The Rose Cross claimed to communicate with God through nature. Physicists, doctors, alchemists, philosophers, gold makers, they enthusiastically approached the study of all problems and looked to name all enigmas. On many points, moreover, they were the successors of the men who, eager for knowledge, for several centuries, devoted themselves to the study of the occult sciences, often getting lost in the pursuit of chimeras, frequently being subsumed by the false, but never ceasing, even in their mystical aberrations, to make a commendable effort to conquer the truth.

We can rank among the Rose Cross forerunners such illustrious men as Roger Bacon, Arnauld de Villeneuve, Raymond Lulle, Henri-Conreille Agripa de Nettesheim, and Aurèle-Philippe-Théophraste Paracelse. Among the Rose Cross themselves we find Michel Maier, physician to Holy Roman Emperor Rudolf II, who was himself an alchemist, Robert Fludd, Jean-Baptiste Van Helmont, John Booker, William Lilly, Thomas Vaughan, Sir Robert Murray, Elie Ashmole, François-Mercure Van Helmont, son of Jean-Baptiste Van Helmont, and Jean-Frédéric Helvétius, doctor to the Prince of Orange and great-grandfather of Claude-Adrien Helvétius.

We have seen that Sir Robert Murray and Elie Ashmole are directly related to the history of Freemasonry.

CHAPTER III

THE EXPANSION OF FREEMASONRY

I

IN HIS EXCELLENT WORK, *THE HISTORY OF FREEMASONRY*, Robert Freke Gould observed that it has mistakenly been considered surprising that Freemasonry had firmly established itself in the most remote parts of Europe a mere ten to twenty years after the creation of the Grand Lodge of England. He finds a natural explanation for this rapid expansion in England's great power, which at that time attracted the attention of the civilised world. "Thanks to the brilliant actions of the Duke of Marlborough", he said, "Great Britain showed its strength to the peoples of the continent; while the other European countries were impoverished by wars, Britain was saved from the suffering and had been able to enrich itself. The possession of Hanover put Britain in contact with Germany; all States there sought alliance and subsidies. London was visited by thousands of foreigners: they wanted to learn what a Grand Lodge was; they then returned to their homeland where they wanted to introduce the Masonic institution." These considerations alone make some of the causes seem clear, but the truth lies elsewhere. As has been said, the 18th century was essentially the "century of the Spirit", the century of "free thought".

Everywhere there was a vast movement towards the ideals of freedom, equality and fraternity. The lodges offered a most precious and useful instrument to this movement; they attracted to their temples all those who wanted to break with the past, abolish abuse, and found a society based on principles of justice that responded to their generous desires and noble aspirations. Isn't the greatest praise we have given to the Masons the words of John Robison, who, believing he would harm them, said: "Reason is the Sun that illuminates the whole, and Liberty and Equality are the objects of their occupations"?

We have recalled which were the first workshops installed outside Great Britain and Ireland, by the Grand Lodge of England. Let us now draw attention to further, equally interesting examples.

On 3rd April, 1732, a lodge was created in Paris; the following year, a lodge was opened in Valenciennes and a lodge was established at the castle of Aubigny, where resided Charles Lennox, Duke of Richmond, and former Grand Master of the Grand Lodge of London. Many initiations took place in "temporary" lodges presided over by English Masonry dignitaries. On 7th September, 1734, a London newspaper reported that, in a lodge held in Paris in the hotel of the Duchess of Portsmouth, the Duke of Richmond, attended by various personages including Montesquieu, performed the acceptance of several neophytes belonging to the highest French nobility. On 20th September, 1733, the same journal reported on another Mason meeting, in which featured the Duke of Richmond, Jean Theophile Desaguiliers, Montesquieu and the latter's friend, Lord Waldegrave, ambassador of His Royal Majesty. In 1737, another London newspaper said that the order of Freemasons "which had long existed in England" was viewed very favourably in Paris, and that very recently eighteen to twenty members of the aristocracy had been initiated.

At that time, Paris was above all the centre of intrigue of the advocates of the Stuarts.

James Francis Edward Stuart, son of James II, commonly called the Knight of St George or even The Old Pretender, proclaimed himself king under the name of James III of England and James VIII of Scotland; in 1715, he attempted an uprising in Scotland, but was forced to return to France. In July 1743, his son, Charles Edward, known as the Young Pretender, approached Scotland, armed, to claim the throne; after a series of alternating successes and setbacks, he suffered an irremediable defeat at Culloden in April 1746. For thirty years, alongside the overt operations, there were all kinds of conspiracies and enterprises. It is due to the efforts of the Jacobites and their incessant propaganda against the British government that there exists a long accredited but erroneous account linking the introduction of Freemasonry in France with the creation of higher ranks.

An article by astronomer Lalande published in 1773 in the *Encyclopaedia* contributed to the spread of misinformation about the creation of the first lodges on French territory. "Around 1725", it was written, "Mylord Dervent-Waters, the knight Maskelyne, M. d'Heguerty and some other Englishmen established a lodge in Paris, on the Rue Des Boucheries, at the home of Hure, an English caterer; in less than ten years, the reputation of this lodge attracted 500 or 600 brothers to Masonry and other lodges were established."

The error is instantly apparent, if one considers that the English lodges were, as we have already indicated, essentially hostile to the supporters of the Stuarts who represented reaction in politics and intolerance in religion. If the slightest doubt could arise on this subject, to dispel it one need only reread the passage of the *Constitutions* in which James Anderson, speaking on behalf of the Freemasons, makes an enthusiastic eulogy of the established order of things. "And now", he writes, "the *Freeborn* BRITISH NATIONS, disentangled from foreign and civil Wars, are enjoying the good Fruits of Peace and Liberty". Is it conceivable that these same lodges were now happy to confer the Masonic quality to men who dreamt of destroying the existing government, who fought with weapons in their hands and who shrank not even from the call abroad?

A German writer, Wilhelm Begemann, adds to these arguments. Charles Radcliffe, Earl of Derwentwater, whose name became Dervent-Waters in Lalande's account, and Hector Maclean, whose name became Maskelyne in that same account, were devoted supporters of the Stuarts. The first was condemned to death by English judges and was beheaded in London in 1746. The second was arrested in Edinburgh in 1743 and thrown in prison. Is it possible that these enthusiastic Jacobites asked for initiation into the lodges whose fundamental maxims went against the very ideas which they defended at the cost of their lives? Another inaccurate version, as we shall see, is that according to which Andrew Michael Ramsay, to whom one attributes the formation of numerous ranks, was nothing but the Pretender's docile agent and worked only in that gentleman's political interest.

Here, reality is, all in all, more fascinating than fiction: it shows us Masonry penetrating France under the patronage of Montesquieu. Must it not be mentioned that he stayed in England from November 1729 until April 1731 and was a friend of Lord Chesterfield, Lord Waldegrave and the Duke of Montagu, members and dignitaries of Freemasonry?

In 1737, five lodges existed in Paris; by 1741, there were twenty-two. The proliferation occured little by little in the provinces; it did not take long to bear fruit. In 1732, one lodge, *L'anglaise*, was formed in Bordeaux, probably by English

Masons staying in the city; it does not seem that it obtained the constitutional letters. By 1740, there were lodges in Lyon, Rouen, Caen, Nantes, Montpellier, and Avignon.

In 1738, the Duke of Antin was named Grand Master for life; in 1743, he was succeeded by prince du sang, Henri de Bourbon, Count of Clermont, whose management was rightly criticised. In the 1743 election, the prince of Conti and the Marshal of Saxony had several votes. In 1773, the Grand Mastery was conferred to another prince du sang, the Duke of Chartres, who, in 1783, upon the death of his father, took the title of Duke of Orléans.

It should be noted of Count Goblet d'Alviella that the Grand Lodge of London was not alone in providing letters for the constitution of lodges on the European continent; the Grand Lodge of Edinburgh established lodges in France, in the United Provinces, in the Austrian Netherlands, in Prussia, in Denmark, and in Russia.

We have seen that in 1731, a temporary lodge was held in The Hague by Lord Chesterfield, Ambassador of King George II to the Estates General, to initiate the Duke of Lorraine. The Grand Lodge of London had given full powers to the Chesterfield brothers, Jean-Theophile Desaguiliers, John Stanhope and Jean Holtzendorff. François, Duke of Lorraine, who in 1736 married Maria Theresia, daughter of Emperor Charles VI, and who in 1737 became Grand Duke of Tuscany, in 1745 was elected Emperor. Workshops soon opened in a few other cities.

It seems that in Germany the first lodges were founded by Germans who had been initiated in England and who had obtained the authorisation to form new workshops. There was a lodge in Hamburg from 1733. Lodges were created from 1740 onwards in Leipzig, Breslau, Altenburg, Frankfurt, Hanover, Bremen and other cities. An important event in the history of German Masonry was the initiation of the Royal Prince of Prussia who was to occupy the throne under the name of Friedrich II. The ceremony took place in Brunswick on the nights of 14th and 15th August, 1738. The prince was accepted by brothers from the Hamburg lodge. When, two years later, he became king, Friedrich expressed a most vivid zeal for the Masonic institution; he founded a lodge in Charlottenburg and presided over its sessions; he showed an ardent proselytism; among those inducted into the new lodge were Prince Wilhelm, the king's brother, Prince Karl Friedrich of Prussia, the Duke of Holstein, and the Margrave of Brandenburg- Bayreuth. The latter set up a lodge in his castle at Bayreuth and another lodge in the city of Bayreuth. Moreover, the Masonic movement spread greatly throughout Germany. Princes, nobles, soldiers, scientists, and the bourgeoisie entered the lodges. The universities also provided neophytes; in 1743, a student lodge was constituted in Halle; shortly afterwards, lodges were created in Iéna and Gœttingue where teachers and students were admitted.

Vienna housed a lodge from 1742; when, in 1745, the brother François of Lorraine was granted imperial dignity, he protected Masonry in his states; the emperor died in 1765; from that date onwards, Maria Theresia was hostile towards the lodges.

It has been argued that a lodge was founded at Mons in 1721. It is said that the Duke of Montagu, Grand Master of the Great Lodge of London, granted the letters of constitution. The arguments proposed to substantiate this theory are insufficient and one consideration in particular must rebuff them. Indeed, if, on 24th June, 1721, the Duke of Montagu had authorised the creation of *La parfaite union*, it would be mentioned in the "official lists" that the Grand Lodge of London published from 1724 in which all the workshops were accounted for with which it was affiliated or itself had created. However, Masonic proliferation did not take long to occur in the Austrian Netherlands. One may cite in particular the effect this point of view had on the war, on the Belgian territory, Great Britain and France; workshops were thus established, depending on the English Masonic authorities, others on the French Masonic authorities; subsequently their founders were English Masons or French Masons, some lodges receiving their constitution letters from the Grand Lodge of Edinburgh. In 1748, the Count of Clermont, national Grand Master of France, founded in Mons the *Vraie et parfaite harmonie* which later became the great provincial lodge of the Austrian Netherlands and which became, in 1770, affiliated with the Grand Lodge of England. Between 1760 and 1780, the activity redoubled: under the protection of Governor General Charles de Lorraine, brother of the emperor François I and, like him, a Freemason. Workshops opened in Bruges, Alost, Brussels, Mechelen, Antwerp, Tournai, Namur, Louvain, Ostend, and other cities.

Several Englishmen founded a lodge in Geneva in 1737. From 1739, there was a lodge in Lausanne; *La parfaite union des étrangers*. In Neuchatel in 1743 the *Aux trois étoiles flamboyantes* lodge was established, under the protection of Frederic II.

Lord Charles Sackville, son of the Duke of Dorset, formed a lodge in Florence in 1736. The Grand Duke François de Lorraine, a Mason as we have just recalled, could not prevent the Inquisition from carrying out their operations at the expense of the members of the workshop.

A lodge opened in Rome in 1735; it was composed of Englishmen but, after two years, it had to halt operations when faced with threats from the Inquisition.

In Naples, a lodge was established in 1745.

In Madrid, the Duke of Wharton, former Grand Master of the Grand Lodge of London, created a lodge on 15th February 1728. He had not obtained any letters of constitution, but the irregularity disappeared when, on 19th March, 1729, the Grand Lodge of London granted the required authorisation. On 9th March 1729, the Grand Lodge of London installed a lodge in Gibraltar which consisted of English officers of the garrison. The proliferation spread to several Spanish cities, and workshops were opened in Cadiz, Barcelona and Valladolid. The Madrid Lodge became a Grand Lodge in 1757.

In Portugal, lodges were also formed.

Freemasonry penetrated Denmark in 1743.

Distinguished personages, who had been initiated either in England or in France, took zealous action in Sweden, that of Axel Eric Wrede being of particular note. In 1753, King Adolphe-Frederic founded a lodge in Stockholm. From 1759, Sweden saw the establishment of a Freemasonry system in which the high ranks were adopted, and which was placed under the invocation of St Andrew, as opposed to the Freemasonry of St John, guardian of the Symbolic ranks.

In Poland, lodges existed from 1739. It was in that same year that King Augustus III authorised the publication of Pope Clement XVII's edict in his states condemning Freemasonry, and forbade the meetings of members of the society. Three years later, new lodges were built.

It has been proven that a lodge was created in Saint Petersburg in 1750; however little information is available on the Masonry situation in Russia before the accession of Catherine II in 1762. We know that the imperatrix looked on the institution favourably for the majority of her reign and that, if she witnessed the hostility that began in 1794, there was however no persecution. She gave herself the honour of guardianship, in her own words, of the *Clio* lodge in Moscow. In 1794, the number of workshops rose to 15.

Paul I ascended to the throne in 1796 and proved himself the adversary of secret societies. His successor, Alexander I, tolerated the spread of Masonry from 1803, but then initiated a period of intense activity that ended with the emperor's order on 12th August 1822. It forbade the Russian Freemasons from any contact or correspondence with their brothers abroad and ordered the closure and dissolution of the lodges. Even today, Freemasonry is banned in Russia. Does it not inscribe on its banners the words of freedom and fraternity and should it not therefore incur the hatred of despotism? By entering into the State's service as civil servants or as officers, the tsar's subjects commit themselves by an oath taken on the Gospel never to be part of a secret society nor of Freemasonry.

The "official lists" of the Grand Lodge of London attest that, from the earliest years, lodges were created in the English colonies of America. In 1729, letters of constitution authorised the installation of a workshop at Trenton in the colony of New Jersey, but no such action was taken; in 1730, Daniel Cox obtained from the Duke of Norfolk, Grand Master of the Grand Lodge of London, complete authority to act as his lieutenant in the colonies of New York, New Jersey and Pennsylvania. The Pennsylvania Lodge was established in 1731; it first purported to be a Grand Lodge, that is, to exist as an independent Masonic lodge, but after a few years it settled to functioning as a large provincial lodge; from 1731 to 1738 it had about fifty members; from 1735 to 1738 it had Benjamin Franklin as its secretary. The Boston Lodge appears, under the date of 31st August, 1733, in the "official lists". Subsequently workshops were opened in most cities of some importance.

In 1763, Canada was established as an English colony; from that time, Masonry was propagated there.

We have seen that, while barely formed, the Grand Lodge of London created workshops in Africa and Asia; it can be generally said that all countries subjected to Great Britain's outreach immediately became the theatre of an ardent proselytism: soldiers, civil servants and colonists made many workshops into centres from which the European influence radiated.

Certain conditions provided the perfect environment for the development of the Masonic institution. Even without the letters of constitution conferred by a regular Masonic authority, the brothers' activity was legitimate; initially five Masons, later seven, had the right to form a lodge and proceed to initiations; by necessity, the lodges were thus made "just, perfect and regular". Accordingly, new workshops were borne of these lodges, either by sending commissioners to carry out the setup, or by distributing copies of their own constitution documents. Decentralisation also led to serious inconveniences: it may be held accountable for the various kinds of difficulties that had to be tackled in the middle of the 18th century. It should not be forgotten that at one point, some lodges were even the "property" of individuals who tampered with initiations and graduation ceremonies. A concerted effort, a solemn claim of the rights of the Grand

Lodges as constituting the only Masonic powers, ended up remedying the evil.

II

MASONRY HAS A UNIVERSAL CHARACTER; IT DOES NOT ABSOLVE its members of their duties towards the homeland, but it teaches them that above the homeland there is humanity; it preaches brotherhood among men and between peoples; thus, by its essence, it is the enemy of war, and when its efforts to preserve peace fail, it uses any means to make international struggles less bloody and to penetrate the hearts of combatants with feelings of commiseration. To this latter end, it exerted its beneficial influence through the creation of military lodges. Not content with spreading its teaching only through the lodges which welcomed all men of good will, Masonry installed special workshops for the officers of the land and sea forces.

The military lodges were mobile, they were *ambulatory lodges*; established in the garrison towns in peacetime, in wartime there were outfits in the camps or on conquered territory. They were not limited to land forces; there are some examples of lodges sitting aboard warships, known as *sea lodges*.

The first military lodge dates back to 1728; it was created by the Grand Lodge of London for one of the Royal Scots battalions, holding garrison on the coast of Coromandel. A second military lodge dates back to 1729, founded by the Grand Lodge of London for the troops of the fortifications of Gibraltar. In 1732, a new military lodge was formed, this time under the Grand Lodge of Ireland. Soon the number of military workshops grew considerably; all in all, by the middle of the

18th century, twenty-nine operated under the Grand Lodge of Ireland and by the end of the same century, there were one hundred and twelve; others were under the Grand Lodge of England and the Grand Lodge of Scotland. In total, from 1728 until the beginning of the 20th century, 409 military lodges had been erected by the three Grand Lodges of the British Isles.

France, Germany, Austria and other countries followed suit. In 1778, thirty military lodges were formed under the Grand Orient of France; in addition, there were lodges in the Irish regiments that were under the king's control. In 1811, the French armed forces had sixty-nine lodges; of the Empire, moreover, most of the marshals and generals and a large number of officers were part of Freemasonry.

Some of these military lodges deserve a special mention; those that Freemasons, as prisoners of war, installed in the cities or camps where they were held. Such lodges appeared in England and Scotland where there were many French prisoners of war during the 18th and beginning of the 19th centuries; one Masonry historian states the number to be twenty-six. In 1759 and 1760, Austrian, Württemberg and Swedish officers, initiated into Freemasonry, were captive prisoners of war in the Prussian fortress in Magdeburg; they created a workshop which, shortly afterwards, obtained the required permission from a Berlin lodge and became a regular lodge. In 1803, a lodge was formed at the Ninth English Infantry Regiment, with letters of constitution from the Grand Lodge of England; in 1805, a battalion of the regiment was transported to the mainland; the ship sank; the officers and 262 soldiers were taken prisoner by the French and held at Valenciennes; the English Masons continued their lodge work at Valenciennes and had regular outfits until 1814, at the era of the conclusion of peace.

III

Solemn meetings were held with many delegates and the power of the lodges was already evident by the end of the 18th century. In 1778, a national convent of the Gauls was held in Lyon; it had been convened by the Scottish lodges. In 1782, the convent of Wilhelmsbad, attended by brothers from all parts of Germany, was presided over by Duke Ferdinand of Brunswick. In 1785, a universal congress opened in Paris, including Masons from London, Vienna, Turin, Weimar, Stockholm, Saint-Petersburg and Moscow. In the invitation which is addressed "to all Masons of all countries", it reads "this century seems destined by divine wisdom to become the epoch of great revolutions in all human knowledge"; "exact science has been transformed, and political systems themselves have experienced the most unexpected changes". The invitation uses the expression "Republic of Macedonia". It lists the principles that the convent must affirm: the existence of one God, the immortality and immateriality of the soul, and the sorrows and rewards in another life.

IV

Masonry knew how to rise above the level of sects and cults. Tolerance formed the basis of its doctrine; and the conquest of prejudices. However, the admission of the Jews was fought for a long time by the lodges of certain countries; the issue was raised as early as 1746 in the lodge *L'Anglaise* of Bordeaux: it was proclaimed that only Christians could be accepted as Masons. During the 19th century, the same subject was raised. With rare exceptions, the lodges provided the rational solution that the fundamental maxims on indifferentism stood in religious matters.

Racial and ethnic prejudice was repressed early on. In 1775, a Protestant pastor, Prince Hall, founded the *African lodge* of black people in Boston. It was Prince Hall who, in 1776, admitted that the free black people could join the revolutionary army. It is true that he failed in his efforts to have the same right recognised for black slaves. After the conclusion of peace, the Grand Lodge of England recognised the *African lodge* and thus made it a "just, perfect and regular" lodge.

CHAPTER IV

FREEMASONRY AND ITS ADVERSARIES

I

FROM THE VERY START OF ITS EXPANSION INTO CONTINENTAL Europe, Freemasonry endured police harassment in some countries, and violent and bloody persecutions in others; it was also exposed to attacks and slander.

In the United Provinces, from 1734 the authorities began to show their resentment; however, they soon noticed that the lodges did nothing to disturb the public peace.

In Paris, a sentence was handed down by the Chatelet's police department on 14th November 1737 forbidding the Freemasons to assemble, but the prohibition had little effect; likewise, when, in 1742, Guyenne's intendant wanted to prevent the *L'Anglaise* lodge in Bordeaux from holding meetings, a mere change of premises sufficed to settle the members' worries.

The Catholic Church held a true hatred for the institution. About thirty years ago, an English magazine, *The Masonic Magazine*, posed the question of what the motives were for such an attitude. "The reason for Rome's hostility", it reads, "is that freedom and equality have always prevailed among the Masons, in the propensity of Freemasonry to encourage the love of science and the search for truth, in the law of charity, in the efforts it has made to unite men of different beliefs in a common cause, finally, in its repudiation of a religion without heart in any form." In addition to these motives, there is one more decisive than the rest: as a secular institution, Masonry directly contests the ecclesiastical hierarchy in favour of humanity.

The first condemnation pronounced by the Holy See against Freemasonry dates from 28th April, 1738, when Clement XII disseminated the papal bull *In eminenti*. The Pope forbade all worshippers to partake in "societies, assemblies or associations under the name of *liberi muratori* or Freemasons, or under any other name, according to the language of the country"; he struck any offenders with the penalty of excommunication. He attempted to justify the action he was taking. "These associations", he said, "have been regarded in the same way in other nations as in ours, since the authorities of different countries have long condemned them as dangers to State security and have cautiously abandoned them". On 14th July 1739, a declaration from the cardinal secretary of state made it known that the bull was to be interpreted in the sense that it was forbidden for Masons to meet anywhere, under penalty of death. In some Catholic countries, the bull was published with the consent of the civil authorities. In other countries, it did not obtain approval; such was the case in France, where it was never considered compulsory.

On 18th May 1751, Benedict XIV renewed the condemnation in the *Providas* bull. In turn, he tried to find motivation for his decision. He relied on the fact that Freemason meetings included persons belonging to different religions; he emphasised that the association established a close bond, and, noting that it was clandestine, he concluded that the institution should be deemed criminal. "The prince and the magistrates", he said, "have the right to know what their subjects do in any assembly, and to prevent the evil they might commit". As a

Masonic author observed, by reproaching Masons for the secrecy with which they surrounded themselves, the Holy See forgot that nascent Christianity had had its own mysteries and initiations which the pagans had made criminal. Unlike *In eminenti*, *Providas* was not published in France.

Almost all the successors to Clement XII and Benedict XIV believed that they had to renew the defences made in these bulls; these include Pius VII, Leo XII, Pius VIII, Gregory XVI, Pius IX and Leo XIII.

It should be noted, however, that in the second half of the 18th century there were many Catholic priests in the lodges; a writer was able to draw up lists for Germany, Austria and France, containing more than 400 people, many of whom held important positions in the Church.

It is true that in some countries, the inquisition managed to apply the bulls of condemnation. We are not referring to the Papal States or Avignon. But in Florence, in 1739, despite the Grand Duke François of Lorraine, himself a Mason, as we have seen, the Holy Office pursued the members of the lodge in one last effort: Thomas Crudeli was thrown in prison; other brothers were tortured.

In the Kingdom of the Two Sicilies, in Spain and in Portugal, Masonry was cruelly persecuted several times. In 1740, Spanish Masons were sent to the galleys; even in 1825, seven members of a lodge in Granada were thrown into dungeons, bound in chains; after a trial, they were condemned to the gallows. In Portugal, brother Jean Coustos was sent to the galleys in 1743, and it took the intervention of the English government to save him; in the same country, rigorous persecution was attempted in 1776.

Already, however, Masonry could name some of its members with pride. In 1747, the *Défense apologétique des francs-maçons* mentioned Emperor Francis I, Prince Charles of Lorraine, brother of the Emperor, King Frederic II, and the Prince of Wales; it noted that almost all the German princes were members of the lodges; the text recalled that Henri de Bourbon, Count of Clermont, was Grand Master of French Masonry with the consent of King Louis XV; it added that in France itself, the most important figures in court had been initiated. "In this great kingdom", it reads, "there is no city of any importance where the Masonic order does not possess a temple and does not count among its members the most distinguished men in the parliaments and in the courts, in the order of nobility, in the order of the clergy and even among the Jesuits".

II

STRONG ATTACKS WERE MADE AGAINST FREEMASONRY THROUGH the press.

In 1730 a booklet which we have already quoted, *Masonry dissected,* appeared in London. The author, Samuel Prichard, said that he was a member of a lodge: he accused the whole institution of deism and even atheism; he doubted the fidelity of Masons and their submission to royal power. The text was frequently reprinted. It gave rise to refutations, at least one of which merits attention.

The refutation to which we allude appeared in a famous book: Volume IV of the *Religious Ceremonies and Customs of All the Peoples of the World,* published in Amsterdam in 1736.

Some passages from a note in this book are interesting. It is first mentioned that the Dutch authorities banned the "Freemason's Society", noting that this society has long existed in the kingdoms of Britain, under the protection of the greatest lords, including the princes of the royal family. Some information is given: the brotherhood tried to form two or three colonies in Holland and to establish lodges there; even in England it remained undisturbed, so that in 1735 there were up to 129 lodges, both in London and in the provinces of England and even outside the kingdom. "One of the rules of confraternity," the note reads, "is to see each other as brothers and assist each other, communicate their insights and opinions, their science, their scholarship and their advice. It is certain that the confraternity is composed of lords, dukes and peers, jurisconsults, doctors, theologians, craftsmen and even thieves. The most illustrious and the richest pay their admission or, if one wishes, their initiation proportionately to their wealth, but it costs less for those of average means, and even less for those of the lowest class, who pay only six or seven shillings."

In *Masonry dissected*, Prichard recounted the legend of Hiram, the questions and answers in the initiation ceremony and the layout of the oath. *Religious Ceremonies and Customs* also contains the oath layout and they note, according to the "official lists" of which we had the opportunity to speak, a list of 129 lodges.

CHAPTER V

HIGH RANKS

I

IN HIS SCHOLARLY WORK ON THE ORIGINS OF THE RANK OF Master, Count Goblet d'Alviella shows that at the beginning of the 18th century, there was only one initiation ceremony for speculative Masons, only one level; after the 1717 formation of the Grand Lodge of London, two levels were created by restoring the rank of apprentice as a fresh starting point; a third level was introduced and spread gradually from 1725; the presence of three ranks was only sanctioned by the Grand Lodge in 1738; it was still not universally accepted in England in 1757.

Towards the middle of the 18th century, the introduction of high ranks began. At this time several historical problems arose that have not yet been resolved satisfactorily. The creation of high ranks has been attributed by many writers to André-Michel Ramsay; it has been suggested that its purpose was to aid the recovery of the Stuarts; the high ranks themselves have been approved by some and violently criticised by others.

A historian of Masonry, Findel, who always declared himself an opponent of the high ranks, recounts one version of the story of their origin. According to him, the supporters of the Old Pretender, James Francis Edward Stuart, had noticed how difficult it would be to push politics into English and Scottish Masonry and, to overcome the difficulty, they had devised a plan to reunite all the faithful supporters of the proscribed royal family in the high ranks. The most favourable ground for the execution of a similar project was France or rather Paris. Ramsay was a speaker in a lodge in this city. "Thus," writes Findel, "when secret propaganda had laid the appropriate groundwork, Ramsay skilfully proposed during his speech the introduction of the high ranks, whose development, due perhaps to other influences also, brought unforeseen and probably different results than those which had been proposed... In 1742, this so-called Scottish Masonry was introduced in Germany, according to a ritual which much resembled that which was published in Lille in 1749 and 1750; In 1743, according to Thory, the Masons of Lyon established, under the name of Petit Elu, the rank of Kadosh, which represents the vengeance of the Templars."

Other writers go into details about Ramsay's actions and the Masonic role of the Young Pretender, son of James Francis Edward Stuart, and his supporters. They cite Ramsay's 1737 speech, in which he attributed the creation of Freemasonry to the Crusaders, arguing that, since the Holy Wars, the lodges had ceased to be prosperous in Scotland, and coming to the conclusion that it was important to bring the institution back to its original organisation; they affirmed that he introduced a rite of seven ranks and they accused him of wanting to replace the regime of brotherhood with the organisation of an order of knighthood. The writers of whom we speak maintain that the Young Pretender created, in 1747, the rite of the faithful Scots, that he himself founded several lodges, and that he erected a primordial chapter of the Rose Cross in Arras, under the distinctive title of *Scottish Jacobite.*

As we have already seen, concerning the Count of Derwentwater and Hector Maclean, it is unlikely that the Jacobites fulfilled the role attributed to them in the historical accounts of Masonry, nor does it seem that Ramsay made the lodges serve political purposes. Ramsay had converted to Catholicism, thanks to Fenelon, who he counted as a friend; he had been the tutor of the Pretender's two sons; but this mission, which he had accepted at the beginning of 1724, lasted only a few months; he became a suspect in the entourage of James Francis Edward Stuart and, in a fit of dejection, he renounced his position. He was initiated as a Freemason in a lodge in London, probably in 1728, at a time when he had obtained permission from the government of George II to return to England; the view that he had formed of Masonry excluded the idea of using it for plots and political struggles; he came to consider it as an association embracing all peoples and uniting all minds and hearts towards the same goal; he wanted it to constitute "a great intellectual nation", and dreamt of making it an academy of scholars and artists. He even proposed that the lodges gather the necessary funds for the printing of a universal dictionary of sciences. Moreover, judging by a few lines of Montesquieu, the Scottish publicist was not fit to execute the plan he was credited with. "I knew Ramsay," he wrote, "he was a bland man: always with the same flattery; he was like Homer's epithets: all his heroes were of the mildest disposition." As for the Masonic propaganda which suggests the involvement of Prince Charles Stuart and the legend according to which he was the supreme and invisible leader of the order, let us remember that, in 1780, he himself declared in a letter that he was, from the point of view of the secret goings-on, in complete darkness.

The high ranks have stalwart defenders. For them, each degree constitutes a teaching and all the lessons form the ranks of symbolic Masonry, the ranks of each chapter and the ranks of the Supreme Council; the symbolic ranks are those of Entered

Apprentice, The Fellowcraft, and Master Mason; beyond them begin the degrees of the chapter which extend until the 18th degree or degree of Rose Cross; the 19th to the 33rd degree rank refer to the Supreme Council. Undoubtedly, they recognise that at certain points of the 18th century, degrees, rites and systems multiplied in an exploitative way, but they maintain that the high ranks, just as the three symbolic ranks, have a purpose because certain elements were successively introduced into the professional lodges. Symbols, legends, liturgy have historical explanations, they say, since they recall in turn, "the significant religious influences, the renunciation of the orders of knighthood, the solidarity of medieval corporations, and finally the mystical, hermetic current that manifests through the centuries. To be truly beneficial," they add, "to exert a profound influence on its followers, Freemasonry must give them a teaching that summarises, in a series of lessons, the experience garnered from ages passed." To quote some of the phases of integral instruction, the grade of Rose Cross is the affirmation of the freedom of thought; the grade of Prince of Lebanon glorifies work; other ranks revive the orders of knighthood, notably the Order of the Temple and the College of Saints or *Kadosh*, which, according to one tradition, was established among the Templars and possessed a secret doctrine borrowed from the East.

Nevertheless, high ranks were admitted in many countries. Historians believe that in Scotland and England, shortly before 1740, there were chapters discussing the rank of Scottish Master of Saint Andrew. From 1743 onwards, the information spread rapidly across France and Germany. In 1755, Scottish lodges were created in the United Provinces. The rites entered Sweden, where they resulted in, around 1781, the constitution of the Swedish system. The development did not stop there, and in the end, the Ancient and Accepted Scottish Rite or *Ecossisme* was established in almost every country in the world alongside symbolic Masonry.

Efforts were made to unify and simplify, and to bring the numerous ranks back under rites and systems. In 1754, the chapter of *Clermont* was created in Paris, in the name and under the auspices of the Grand Master, the Count of Clermont. In 1755, the reform of German Masonry was addressed by the Baron of Hund; it led, in 1767, to the constitution of the Order of Strict Observance; the fundamental idea was that every Freemason be a Templar; Strict Observance was to extend over the whole of Europe, which was divided into nine provinces with their provincial chapters, priories, and commanderies.

Findel notes that in Germany, simplicity and the absence of any complication in the fundamental principles led to the presumption that an important secret lay hidden beneath the emblems; it was concluded that such a secret could only be conferred to a small number of followers belonging to the higher ranks; according to the same writer, Ramsay's speech trying to link the lodges to the crusades served as a starting point for vague hypothesising. The movement gained all the more strength since it was supported by a fraction of French Masonry and since, during the Seven Years' War, many French Masons penetrated Germany in the wake of troops and diplomats.

The ranks increased to 10, 25, 33 and even 95 degrees. Moreover, legends were formed and several illustrious figures were credited with roles they had not fulfilled. This was the case for Frederick II, who, after having adopted a Masonic system comprising 25 grades, was said to have overhauled it in a council held in Berlin on 1st May, 1786. By virtue of the rights conferred on him by his alleged capacity as head of both old and modern Masonry, it was suggested he added 8 grades to the 25 that already existed and instituted a Supreme Council at the 33rd grade, which he himself would have regulated. Historians have shown that the "constitutions and laws" of 1st May 1786 are apocryphal; two of their arguments are key: At that time, Frederick II was no longer taking part in any Masonic activities, and "constitutions and laws" could not have been altered in a council held in Berlin on 1st May, 1786, because, from 17th April, 1786, the King was ill at the castle of Sans-Souci, where he died on 17th August, 1786, without having visited the capital.

II

It is excessively difficult to shed any light on the struggles that occurred between 1740 and 1790 within Masonry in several countries, notably in France and Germany. Many systems were formed in which the love of the wonderful, vanity, the spirit of intrigue and even charlatanism were given free rein. It is true that part of the order continued to adhere to the three symbolic grades, or made only slight concessions to the tendency of imposing higher ranks.

In the book entitled: *Concerning the Prussian Monarchy under Frederick the Great*, written in 1788 in collaboration with Jacob Mauvillon, the Count of Mirabeau devoted several pages to Masonry. "Around this time," he said of the middle of the 18th century, "everyone wanted to become a Freemason; princes especially entered this society in droves. But it became clear that it was no longer possible to run such a large company and they wanted to change direction. Then appeared, as if from out of the earth, they wrote, men sent by unknown superiors and armed with the powers to restore order and return it to its ancient purity." He showed that there was discussion in the lodges of the theory that Masonry was only a continuance of the Order of the Knights Templar; he recounted the evils that were the result of disputes and quarrels and he ended by mentioning the efforts made to constitute an eclectic Masonry that professed tolerance towards all adopted systems.

In a few lines, Findel illustrated the changes that took place in French Masonry. "Every day," he says, "saw a new system emerge. In 1756, the first regular chapter of high ranks in all of France was instituted, that of the Knights of the East, who called themselves the 'sovereign princes of the order'; over the course of 1758, a new system appeared comprising 25 different ranks, which was pompously entitled 'Council of Eastern and Western Emperors', and whose members were called the 'sovereign Mason princes'. This last system distributed rules of constitution for lodges of higher grades, it appointed inspectors and deputies for the propagation of this so-called 'raised and perfect Masonry' across Europe, and in France it founded several 'particular councils'." We can add that the evil was aggravated by circumstances at that time; in several countries on the continent, some lodges were the property of these Venerables who went so far as to tamper with initiations and graduation ceremonies.

In order to remedy the perilous situation, cautious negotiations were necessary; in the countries where the discord had been unleashed, it was also necessary to consider establishing some central authority.

In Paris, with the consent of the provincial Masons, the "great English lodge in France" had been formed around 1743, and in 1756 took the name of "Grand Lodge of France"; it was composed of the Venerables who presided over the regular lodges of Paris and had at its head the Grand Master and his representatives. Recognising only the three symbolic grades, the lodge saw its authority challenged by the colleges, chapters and councils of the higher grades.

Some systems claimed to bring new spirit to Freemasonry. One was *Martinesisme,* originating from Martinez de Pasqually, which became Martinism when Louis-Claude de Saint-Martin joined, giving the system new strength. It was a mixture of Freemasonry, mysticism and occult sciences; it recognised ten ranks which, in the minds of the founders, would lead followers back to the acquisition of almost supernatural powers; it proclaimed itself to be Christian, but struggled against priestly domination. "It is the ignorance and hypocrisy of the priests which is one of the main causes of the evils which have afflicted Europe for several centuries until today," writes Saint-Martin.

Another system, that of the *Philalèthes* or *Amis de la Vérité* [Friends of Truth], exerted considerable influence in France and neighbouring countries. Created in Paris, it entered into close relationships with several provincial lodges, notably with the lodge of the *Chevaliers bienfaisants* [Beneficent Knights] of Lyon, and it extended its correspondence to various foreign countries. The *Philalèthes* managed the convocation of the convents that was held in Paris in 1785 and 1786. The board of brothers who were summoned to these meetings bore witness to the ideas of cosmopolitanism which already reigned; these were Johann Joachim Christoph Bode, court counsellor in Weimar, the margrave of Anspach and Bayreuth, Baron Dalberg of Manheim, Jean-Jacques Duval d'Eprémesnil, *conseiller* in the *parlement* of Paris, Duke Ferdinand of Brunswick, the Marquis of Gages, Grand Master of the provincial Grand Lodge of the Austrian Netherlands,

Prince Louis of Hesse-Cassel, Prince Frédéric of Hesse-Darmstadt, Jean-Gaspar Lavater and Diethelm Lavater of Zurich, Anne of Montmorency, the Duke of Luxembourg, the Prince of Nassau, the Duke of Rochefoucauld, Louis-Claude de Saint-Martin, officer of the *Régiment de Foix*, and Count Alexandre Strogonoff, the Russian Ambassador.

III

DISSENT AROSE WITHIN THE GRAND LODGE OF FRANCE. SOME energetic men resolved to form a new central body while retaining a legitimate share of control in the various lodges; amongst them were Anne of Montmorency, the Duke of Luxembourg and the famous astronomer Jérôme Lalande. Delegates from the lodges gathered in Paris in 1772 and in the first months of 1773: their meeting bore the characteristic title of "National Assembly". The deliberations led to the formation of the *Grand Orient*. "It was not", writes Louis Amiable, "a simple change of name and people. The new organisation fully imparted a representative character to the central body, inviting the deputies of the provincial lodges to sit with those of Parisian lodges, and dissipating the abuse of the irremovable Venerables, in a way the owners of their lodges, abuse which invalidated the Parisian ateliers. In addition, a general purification of the Masonic personnel was carried out by means of the obligation imposed on all the lodges to be reconstituted by the central authority." From 1773 onwards, there was an organisation in France which could truly serve as a model for the very constitution of the nation and which functioned like a monarchical and parliamentary government. The Grand Master, who was the Duke of Chartres, had taken an oath before the Grand Orient; the Grand Orient had two hundred and fifty-seven deputies belonging to the nobility, the clergy, the liberal professions, the judiciary, the army, the bank and industry. From that point on, each lodge had to elect its Venerable and dignitary officers. Sixteen years before the Revolution, it was the establishment of the liberal regime.

The creation of the Grand Orient did not dissolve the Grand Lodge of France: the two "powers" competed; but the Grand Orient had the benefit of exercising the most fervent influence. Opposite the Grand Orient and the Grand Lodge of France, the great general chapter of France was maintained by the merger of the Council of Eastern and Western Emperors and the Knights of the East. Let us add that in 1786, the Grand Orient adopted four high ranks, those of Elu, Knight of the East, Scottish Knight and Rose Croix.

In Germany, Masons who wanted to restore peace to the members of the lodges created the *Eklektischer Bund* [Eclectic Alliance] in 1783. "Freedom and equality", it was said in the invitation newsletter, "being the basis on which the foundations of our society have raised this edifice, which does so much to honour humanity, have been strongly shaken by internal divisions, despotism, Egoism and the spirit of sedition. It is necessary to unite all our forces to restore to Masonry its original dignity and restore, by the bonds of friendship, the closest fraternal union that once existed between the brothers. Let us preserve, in the presence of the profane world, as well as the Masonic world, a prudent neutrality with regard to all the systems known up to now, none of which has yet been sufficiently established or is likely to be, and let us eliminate all that could make us suspicious to the civil authority. Any lodge may keep all its own higher grades which are not the general case, but first of all, let us restore true Masonry on its former footing, before the appearance of all these new systems." The fundamentals of the alliance were the following: only the three Masonic grades were uniformly recognised for all allied lodges; each lodge was free to introduce higher grades, but these would not become common to the whole order; all the allied lodges were equal; the provincial lodges of Wetzlar and Frankfurt formed a board of directors. In 1789, the Eclectic Alliance comprised thirty German lodges.

CHAPTER VI

THE ILLUMINATI

In Germany, 1776, the order of the Illuminati was founded. The founder was Adam Weishaupt, professor of Canon Law and practical philosophy at the University of Ingolstadt in Bavaria. Mirabeau describes the goal that the members of this new secret association pursued: "They were following Jesus' order," he said, "but proposing diametrically opposed views. The Jesuits want to chain men to the altars of superstition and despotism; the enlighteners believed that by using the same means, prudence, time, perseverance, they could turn against their opponents with the advantage of having no external ritual... no visible leader... and thus nothing would be missing to enlighten men and make them happy and free."

"Weishaupt," writes Findel, "used his position as a teacher and the favour he had gained to form a party. Clearly, he could not do it in the open. He gathered his audience under the pretext of a rehearsal, and exposed to them the result of his philosophical research; he engaged them to read Bayle and other authors, and trained them to consider the events of the period with a critical eye. Then, he urged them to exercise a great deal of prudence and discretion, and he promised them a higher degree of enlightenment and called them Illuminati." Important persons belonging to the administration, to the teaching, to the Church, were also affiliated and became the most active collaborators in the work. In 1777, Weishaupt was accepted into a Mason lodge in Munich, and he decided to push the association he had just created onto Freemasonry and to take advantage of the help it could offer him.

The order of the Illuminati had many ranks; the upper classes remained totally hidden from the followers of the lower classes. Absolute secrecy was obligatory, and mysterious initiations ensured that the members be both devoted and intelligent. But the institution had the serious defect of being despotic and allowing mutual surveillance and spying amongst the followers.

The fundamental ideas were the improvement of man and the destruction of the abuse that had been introduced into society; the means was for members to penetrate public office, and by the same measure, seize control over the State. Illuminism preached equality and freedom which, according to its doctrine, were the essential rights that man in his original perfection is given by nature; it showed how the right of property infringes on equality, and how governments, the sole endorser of property, infringe on freedom...; he offered to deliver people from the tyranny of princes and priests; to make immediate progress, he wanted the liberation of workers and peasants in Germany, which was doomed to despotism: no more serfdom, no more drudgery, no more trade; such was the preliminary reform.

Thanks to the work of some of Weishaupt's collaborators, notably Adolphe of Knigge, Baader, Xavier Zwack, the Marquis of Constanza, and Count Savioli, nearly two thousand members were brought to the cause. To better ensure secrecy, affiliates bore names generally borrowed from ancient history. Weishaupt was called Spartacus, Knigge was Philon, Baader was called Celse, Zwack was called Cato, Constanza was called Diomedes, and Savioli was Brutus. There were princes in the association; Ernest II, Duke of Saxe-Coburg and Gotha, Karl August, Grand Duke of Saxe-Weimar-Eisenach and Charles William Ferdinand, Duke of Brunswick. The sect spread throughout Germany. Weishaupt established a centre of propaganda in Paris which, although it did not become all-powerful, was not without influence. In Switzerland, Poland, and Russia, there were many members.

Dissent occurred between the main leaders, and allowed the Bavarian government to become aware of the Illuminati's operations. Police investigations, seizure of important documents, and the arrest of numerous members, were many successive blows to the association in the first months of 1784. "The government", said Mirabeau, "struck Count Savioli, who was sent back to Italy with a very modest pension. Weishaupt, professor at Ingolstadt, was hunted along with several others. They were imprisoned, and thrown into the convents to do penance; finally, except for death and bodily torment, these unfortunate men suffered everything." "The Munich government's procedure in this whole affair", Mirabeau adds, "has been outrageous and tyrannical; however, remarkably, the sword has not been dared to be used, so powerful is the spirit of the century."

Adam Weishaupt found asylum against persecution in the lands of Duke Ernest II, who appointed him as court councillor. He died in Gotha, in 1830, at the age of 83.

We have mentioned the names of some followers of Illuminism; other names may be noted; those of Goethe, Herder and Georg Friedrich von Martens, professor of human rights at the University of Göttingen, all three of whom also belonged to Masonry. As for the group formed in Paris, we find Mirabeau, Vazotte, Robespierre and Lavoisier.

Furthermore, let us note, writers with very moderate opinions have not hesitated to pay homage to the efforts of Illuminism. One of them, Redepenning, using notes abandoned by Gieseler, author of the scholarly *Church History*, recognises the services Weishaupt rendered. He admits that many members of the sect were hostile to Christianity and wanted to replace it with deism, but at the same time he declares that they were very useful, especially in Bavaria where they fought against superstition and paved the way for serious reform.

CHAPTER VII

THE FOLLOWERS OF Freemasonry

FINDEL SAYS IT SO VERY WELL: "MASONRY IS THE BROADEST alliance which exists within humanity; it is a vast circle which embraces all the secondary systems by association; there is no other society which has, as its fundamental principle above all else, the greater good." It is therefore not surprising that it has never lacked support and that the most brilliant minds, the most devoted hearts, have been eager to increase the number of its followers. Kings, princes, statesmen, warriors, philosophers, writers and scholars have appeared and still appear on the lodges' lists alongside merchants, industrialists, the bourgeoisie and simple workers. We have already had the opportunity to quote some eminent characters; we will add some brief supplementary information by revisiting special Masonic journals and books devoted to the history of Masonry.

In 1738, by order of the Grand Lodge, a new edition of the 1723 *Constitutions* was published in London; these are the *New Constitutions*, the work of James Anderson. It recounts that Francis II, Duke of Lorraine who, as we saw, had received the grade of Apprentice and Companion in a lodge formed in the Hague in 1731 for that very purpose, the same year obtained the grade of Master in a lodge formed by the Grand Master at the castle of Sir Horace Walpole in Houghton Hall in Norfolk County; it also tells how Frederick, Prince of Wales, became an Apprentice, then a Companion, in an impermanent lodge constituted, on 5th November, 1737, at Kew Palace. In 1743, the Duke of Cumberland, brother of Prince Frederick, was also initiated. From 1737 to 1874, fifteen royal princes of England entered Masonry.

As we have said, Frederick II was initiated in 1738 when he was a royal prince. After being crowned king, he assiduously took part in Masonic operations and presided over the initiation ceremony of several princes. Frederick II gave the testament that the goal of Masonry was to make men more sociable and more beneficent. Responding, on 15th February, 1777, to an address from the Grand Lodge *Royal York zur Freundschaft* [Royal York of Friendship] in Berlin, he wrote these lines: "Your speaker perfectly expressed the spirit which animates all your operations. A society which works only to germinate and bear fruit of all virtues in my States can always count on my protection; it is the glorious duty of any sovereign; I will never stop fulfilling it." All the successors of Frederick II to the throne of Prussia, with the exception of William II, were initiated.

Since Gustav III, the kings of Sweden have been Freemasons and have declared themselves the protectors of Freemasonry.

In Denmark, kings are graced with Grand Mastery.

During the second half of the 18th century and most of the 19th century, several princely families in Germany, such as the houses of Brunswick, Hesse, Saxe-Coburg and Gotha, and Saxe-Weimar, provided zealous and active followers for Masonry.

When the kingdom of the Netherlands was created, William I's two sons became Masons. The Royal Prince Willem Frederik was initiated in 1817 in the *L'Espérance* [Hope] lodge in Brussels; Prince Frederik received the light in the *Zu den drei Weltkugeln* [The Three Globes] lodge in Berlin, and became Grand Master of the Grand Orient of the Netherlands with jurisdiction over the southern provinces.

Need we recall that the first king of the Belgians was a Mason? Initiated at the *L'Espérance* lodge in Berne, on 1st September, 1813, he was awarded the second and third rank three months later. A few years later, he became affiliated with a lodge in London. When, in their festivals, the Belgian Masons drank the health of Leopold I, they also drank to the health of his two sons. They said they had the right and the duty to claim them, because they were *Lowtons* and all they lacked was the Masonic baptism.

We saw that Benjamin Franklin was part of the Philadelphia Lodge from the early days of its foundation. For eight and a half years in Paris he was the plenipotentiary of the United States, which had just shaken the yoke of Great Britain; he assiduously followed the lodges' work; moreover, he was affiliated to the lodge *Les neuf sœurs* [The Nine Sisters] and, in 1779, he became its leader. George Washington was initiated in 1752; in 1797, he became Grand Master of the Lodges of Pennsylvania. He was a devoted and faithful brother. Thomas Jefferson and John Adam were Masons, as were most of the founders of the American republic.

Motesquieu was a Mason. Voltaire was accepted, on 7th April, 1778 in the *Les neuf sœurs* lodge, of which the astronomer Lalande was then Venerable. When he entered the temple, Voltaire was supported by Franklin and Antoine Court de Gébelin. He died on 30th May, 1778; on 28th November, the lodge *Les neuf sœurs* held a funeral ceremony; Lalande occupied the pulpit of Venerable; Franklin and Count Strogonoff were overseers. On the subject of Voltaire, let us recall that, according to one opinion, he was initiated between 1727 and 1729. At that time, he was staying in England, where he had been taken by order of the Lieutenant General of Police, Herault, when on 2nd May, 1727, he left the Bastille. It was noted that, at his reception in *Les neuf sœurs*, he was treated as having already received the symbolic light.

Among the Masons of the United Kingdom are men such as Gibbon, Robert Burns, Walter Scott, Brougham, and Priestley.

Masonic Germany proudly cites the names Herder, Lessing and Goethe. Herder was initiated in May 1766 in the *A l'épée* [To the Sword] lodge in Riga; Lessing was accepted on 14th October, 1771, in the Hamburg Lodge *Zu den drei Goldenen Rosen* [At the Three Gold Roses]; Goethe was initiated on 23rd June, 1780 in the *Amalia* lodge in Weimar. These three illustrious thinkers rendered invaluable services to Masonry; through their writings, they spread its principles; with it they have conquered many new supporters; they have confirmed supporters in their convictions.

Their action was especially beneficial because they showed that the idea of humanity is superior to the ideas of nationality and religion, and they have substituted exclusivity, narrowness and fanaticism with the idea of the human family.

Herder wrote *Ideas upon Philosophy and the History of Mankind* and *Letters for the Advancement of Humanity*; he published works where he was more particularly concerned with Freemasonry. Findel has made an excellent judgment of his work. "The advancement of humanity," he says, "of which he was the apostle, seemed to him to be the most sublime attribute of our species; to devote himself to his fellow man, in whatever way or in whatever place he was oppressed, whether his indigence be physical or moral, was Christianity; according to him, it was the spirit of his doctrine and the motive of life..." This great thought that the human race is in itself susceptible to infinite improvement, and his faith in the future for which it was necessary to prepare, animated all his efforts and were imprinted in each of his writings. "There is only one structure," he tells the true Mason, "that must be built, the simplest and the greatest; it can be heard in every century and in every nation...".

Lessing composed *Dialogues for Freemasons,* where he highlighted the important role of Masonry, a universal association. He says that the meeting of men in societies while uniting individuals is a cause of division, since each of these particular societies has its own interest with which the members of the State identify and which makes the citizens of one state consider as enemies the citizens of other states; he notes that religions exert a similar effect on their followers; the remedy is the organisation of the human race; the means of realising this organisation is Freemasonry. He does not want love of the homeland to manifest itself in hatred of the foreigner and in homicidal war; he opposes feelings of intolerance with the fundamental law of the Masons; he opens their temples to all those who are worthy of being accepted, without concern for the country of origin, worship or civil condition. Libertarian and anarchist, he dreamed of replacing the State with the union of "the noblest and wisest men".

Goethe was initiated in 1780; on 2nd March, 1782, he received the rank of Master at the same time as Grand Duke Karl August. Shortly after, the *Amalia* lodge fell dormant. When operations began again in 1808, he took an active part; this is how he fulfilled the function of orator in 1813 and 1822, and on several occasions, he delivered admirable speeches. In 1813, in particular, he said a eulogy for Wieland, who had been accepted in 1809; on 15th June 1821, in an address, he insisted on the equality of Masons. "Rank, duty, age, fortune, talent, everything disappears", he said, "in unity; everyone occupies the place given to him; the mission of Masonry is humanity and fraternal love, free from the prejudices of race and position and free from the prejudices of a religion that claims to be the only path to salvation." On 23rd June 1830, the *Amalia* lodge celebrated the great man's 50th Masonic birthday. Goethe died on 22nd March, 1832. On 9th November of the same year, a mourning lodge was held in his memory. "The Venerable of the lodge", said Findel, "recalled his work: For more than fifty years, Goethe showed himself constantly devoted to the confraternity of French Masons; especially when the *Amalia* lodge adopted the simple and ancient ritual of the great lodge of Hamburg. He then devoted himself entirely to serving the association and from that point onwards he did not cease to take an immediate role in all important affairs and all formalities."

Fichte, who had probably been initiated in Zurich, was affiliated with the *Royal York of Friendship* lodge in Berlin; but differences of opinion about which reforms were appropriate to be introduced led him to part from this lodge. The famous philosopher devoted special works to Masonry; all his works, moreover, are characterised by the idea of freedom. In this passage from *Reden an die deutsche Nation* [Addresses to the German Nation], he writes of the objections against the consolatory role of religion. "Although it is true," he said, "that religion is, for one thing, the consolation of the unjustly oppressed slave, yet this above all is the mark of a religious disposition, viz., to fight against slavery and, as far as possible, to prevent religion from sinking into a mere consolation for captives. No doubt it suits the tyrant well to preach religious resignation and to bid those look to heaven to whom he allows not the smallest place on earth. But we for our part must be in less haste to adopt this view of religion that he recommends; and we must, if we can, prevent earth from being made into a hell in order to arouse a greater longing for heaven."

Krause was accepted as Mason in the Altenburg lodge *Archimedes zu den drei Reissbrettern* [Archimedes of the Three Tracing Boards]. It was 1805. Soon he became affiliated to the lodge in Dresden *Zu den Drei Schwertern* [At the Three Swords]. Findel said, "Free from the shackles of all foreign authority, expressing only his own conviction, which was the result of his profound and learned research, Krause imposed on himself the task of stimulating with all his power the work of Freemasonry, of dedicating his life to it and of ensuring that the other brothers also consider this institution from a philosophical perspective. Through his key work, *Die drei ältersten Kunsturkunden der Freimaurerbrüderschaft* [The Three Oldest Art Documents of the Masonic Fraternity], he filled a sensitive gap in the history of Masonry and acquired the recognition of the enlightened and thinking part of the confraternity. Together with Ignaz Aurelius Fessler, he laid the foundations for new German Masonic literature and critical history." The work comprises two volumes; the first appeared in 1810, the second in 1813. Krause and Mossdorf, who assisted him, were indicted; they emerged victorious from the first struggle, but soon they were struck with the penalty of expulsion. With reason, Findel blames the lodge and praises the victims. "The devotion and merit of Krause and Mossdorf," he writes, "appear all the greater and more worthy of recognition, when one looks back to the time of their first public acts, when the priceless worth of freedom in advertising and scientific research, that today no one would dare attack, was not yet conquered."

Among the legal advisers who were part of Masonry, we can here quote Johann Kaspar Bluntschli, the author of *Le Droit International Codifié* [International Law Codified] and many remarkable works. Initiated in 1838 in the *Modestia cum libertate* lodge in Zurich, he became affiliated in 1864 with *Ruprecht zu den Fünf Rosen* [Ruprecht of the Five Roses] in Heidelberg; in 1872, he became Grand Master of the Grand Lodge *Zur Sonne* [To the Sun] in Bayreuth. "It was," a Mason said of him, "an ornament and a concealing force of our alliance." We can also quote a man who rendered eminent services to the noble cause of human rights, Gustave Rolin-Jaequemyns, and who was accepted as Mason in the lodge *La Liberté* [Freedom] in Ghent.

Without going into further detail, let us note the initiation of Emile Littré. It took place in Paris on 8th July, 1875, in *La Clémente Amitié* [Clement Friendship]. The ceremony was attended by brothers Louis Blanc, Léon Gambetta, Madier de Montjau, and Challemel-Lacour. Jules Ferry was initiated the same day.

CHAPTER VIII

FREEMASONRY OPERATIONS

I

"FREEMASONRY," SAYS COUNT GOBLET D'ALVIELLA," IS A SECRET association which establishes a bond of brotherhood between free and honourable people that overcomes all distinctions of race, country, class, profession, party and sect."

We have indicated which are the fundamental ideas that it pursues. In all its instructions and at all levels, the Order affirms its will to strive for the advancement of man. "The duty," it is proclaimed, "is to act according to the moral law that teaches: Do unto others as you would have them do unto you." It is glorified work. "Masons only unite together to work, as is expressed in an old manual. Work, the preservative element of man, helps his physical existence and is vital to his moral existence. Work is useful pleasure, and pleasure is pleasant work."

According to legend, Hiram worked for seven years to build a temple that would bring all men together in the same cult, that of truth. "The temple," the instructions say, "is man, it is the human heart; working to perfect the temple means working to improve one's morals, to perfect one's being." The question is posed: does the study of the Masonic grades lead to knowledge of the truth? "No rank," such is the answer, "teaches or reveals the truth; it only thins the veil." Another question concerns secrecy. "The secret of Freemasonry," it is said, "is by its very nature inviolable, because the Mason who knows it can only have guessed it. He discovered it by frequenting the educated lodges, by comparing and judging. Once he has made this discovery, he will keep it for himself, and will not even communicate it to the brother in whom he has the most confidence; because as soon as that act rendered the brother unable to make this discovery himself, he would also lose the power of benefitting from the very secret that had been told to him."

The facts and indications here recalled allow us to show how fruitful Masonic propaganda was in the 18th century; it was even more so in the 19th century. One of the first results was the transformation of public opinion in most countries. The notions of freedom and tolerance permeated almost everywhere; more and more powerful voices rose up to demand the security of a loyal government almost everywhere. There are few countries where the lodge did not gather men of intelligence and who vowed to exercise a happy influence on those around them, and who were capable of guiding them in politics. It can be said, without fear of error, that if the power of public opinion takes on such importance and if, going beyond the limits of the States, it adjudicates today on all the great events which occur in the world, it is owing in major part to the universal organisation of Masonry. As we have already said, there is no political, religious or social question which is not studied and discussed in the lodges; there is no problem of interest to the citizens to any degree which is not the object of examination; the studies and discussions occur away from any pressure of the authorities; the brothers who engage in them have, above the members of any association, the inappreciable advantage of being free of any intellectual constraint.

When, over the course of the last two centuries, reforms were advocated in some part of the globe, they received the unconditional support of Freemasonry; it is even generally through this support that abuses were destroyed and that improvements were introduced in the government and in the legislation of the States.

It is thanks to the support of the Masons, so numerous in Tuscany, that Grand Duke Leopold II managed to realise his projects. He had succeeded to the Grand Duchy in 1765, following his father François I who, as Duke of Lorraine, had been initiated in 1731. We know the main provisions that Peter Leopold introduced into government and administration: the privileges of the nobility were destroyed; equality before the law was demanded; art and craft guilds gave way to the freedom of industry; the gift of tax exemption enjoyed by the clergy disappeared; private jurisdictions were abolished; the prison system was improved; a more gentle criminal code replaced bloody laws; torture and corporal punishment were abolished; from 1765 on, no death sentences were carried out, and on 30th November 1786, the death penalty was abolished.

Joseph II's reforms would probably never have been attempted had it not been for the influence of a group of Masons in Vienna which included Ignaz von Born and Joseph von Sonnenfels; Sonnenfels, professor of administrative sciences at the University of Vienna, and a scholarly publicist, figured as one of the first opponents of the death penalty alongside Beccaria, who had the honour of having convinced Maria Theresia and Joseph II of the need to abolish torture.

When the movement that was to lead to the restoration of human dignity and the destruction of black slavery began, Masonry provided the most ardent source of propaganda. Towards the middle of the 18th century, a Mason, Montesquieu, wrote an admirable page on the slavery of black people in which he invited the princes of Europe to finalise a general convention in favour of mercy and pity. About forty years later, the *Société des amis des Noirs* [Society of the Friends of the Blacks] was founded in Paris; its creators and leaders were members of Masonry: Brissot, Clavier, La Fayette, Mirabeau, and Pétion.

It has been said that the United States is a Masonic creation.[5] The primordial ideas of Freemasonry were affirmed by the glorious founders of the great republic who almost all belonged to the lodges. A hundred years ago, a French Mason, Choslin, orator at *La Constance Couronnée* [Crowned Constance] in Paris, made an observation which, while focusing on one detail, carries a certain interest. He showed that Freemason Franklin was introducing the Masonic principles into the legislation of his country. "To further indicate the influence of our wise institution," he added, "Franklin gave the United States stars on a blue background as seen on the vaults of our temples, and the emblems of Freemasonry float on all seas, a revered flag in the most powerful nations of the world."

Masonry played a dominant part in the philosophical movement that spread throughout the civilised world of the 18th century. "All who thought," wrote Cesare Cantù, "wanted to be affiliated with the lodges; discourse on the boldest philosophy of the time in the secret societies contributed more than a little to the spread of revolutionary ideas."

In a book published in 1797, John Robison, professor at the University of Edinburgh, who had been initiated and who,

5 *Libres entretiens. Union pour la verité*; V. – *Les idées humanitaires*; VI. – *Unification du droit*. Paris, 1906.

during his travels on the continent, visited a large number of lodges, endeavoured to describe the role of Freemasons in what he called conspiracy against all religions and against all governments. Speaking of the French lodges prior to the Revolution, he showed them to be "populated with lawyers, abbots, and so-called philosophers, who discussed all matters of religion and politics." He said, "There is frequent evidence of this in the many speeches of the orator brothers. In a speech given in Lyon in the lodge *Les Chevaliers Bienfaisants* [Beneficent Knights] by brother Robinet, when the Grand Master of the Order, the Duke of Chartres, came to visit, we found the seed and the substance of his famous work: *De la Nature* [Of Nature]. Brother Condorcet gave a speech, in Strasbourg, in the lodge *Les Philalèthes* [Lovers of Truth] where we see the plan of his posthumous work: "*The progress of the human spirit.* A speech by Mirabeau, in *Les Chevaliers Bienfaisants* in Paris, is filled with the principles of equalisation and cosmopolitanism that he so vehemently declared in the tribune of the National Assembly."

Robison highlighted the importance of *Les Chevaliers Bienfaisants,* which was the most zealous of all the cosmopolitan lodges in France and which operated for a long time under the special protection of the Grand Master, the Duke of Chartres. He wrote: "Lodges that became affiliated to it were formed in several cities in France; in Paris, Strasbourg, Lille, and Toulouse. There were quarrels which were somehow calmed by the establishment of new lodges under the name of *Amis réunis de la vérité* [Friends reunited with the truth]. One of the lodges formed in Paris under this name became very famous. The mother lodge, which was in Lyon, extended its connections to Germany and in all the other foreign countries, and sent regulations and systems according to which all the lodges directed their operations." The author recalled that the Munich lodge *Theodor von der guten Rath* [Theodore of the Good Council], which was daughter to the lodge *Les Chevaliers Bienfaisants*, inspired the Bavarian government with great fear through its speeches against religion and against civil authority. He added that another lodge of the same association, which was established in Regensburg, aroused frequent commotions and insurrections, and that the lodges of Lorraine and Alsace, together with those of Spire and Worms, worked in 1791 to facilitate Custine's entry into Germany, and delivered Mentz into his hands.

II

THE ADMISSION OF WOMEN TO THE LODGES LED TO THE formation of the Rite of Adoption.

In 1774, the Grand Orient in France welcomed the new ritual. Every lodge of adoption had to be linked to a regular lodge which took responsibility for it; the attire had to be presided over by the Venerable or by a dignitary officer; all the followers were women, widows or close relatives of Freemasons; there were four ranks: Apprentice, Companion, Mistress, and Perfect Mistress. The meetings were almost always charitable celebrations.

"After the decision of the Grand Orient, taken in the General Assembly of 10th June, 1774," a historian wrote, "a large part of the workshops constituted in the capital and the kingdom, and even foreign lodges, hastened to initiate the wives and daughters of their members by conforming to the rules and forms adopted in Paris and which were received as general laws. These kinds of meetings soon spread to Germany,

Russia, the United Provinces, Italy and elsewhere. England did not partake."

The most remarkable of the lodges of adoption was *La Candeur* [Candour]. We have the register of the minutes of its meetings, from 21st March, 1775, date of the inauguration, until 18th February, 1785. Among the sisters were the Duchess of Chartres, the Princess of Lamballe, the Countess of Polignac, the Countess of Choiseul and almost all the ladies of the court.

III

AT ONE TIME IN THE 18TH CENTURY, THE MASONIC MOVEMENT was extraordinarily intense. A laudatory pamphlet published in 1820 estimated, for the year 1787, that there were 3,315 lodges operating across the globe, with more than 300,000 followers.

In 1777, in France alone, 300 lodges recognised the authority of the Grand Orient; 247 lodges were under the management of the Grand Lodge of France; in the same year, the Grand Orient was in correspondence with 1,200 foreign lodges.

In 1787, the authority of these two Masonic powers was recognised by 636 lodges, 67 of which were established in Paris and 71 attached to regiments.

In 1769, Lalande founded the lodge *Les sciences* [The Sciences], with the aim of grouping together Masons especially devoted to scientific research; on the advice of Helvétius, he undertook to widen the framework and to form a workshop in which scientists, literary writers, and artists would meet.

Thus, in 1776, five years after the death of Helvétius, the lodge *Les neuf sœurs* [The Nine Sisters] was erected. One historian said that each muse was represented there by talented men. On the charts of this noble lodge were inscribed illustrious names: Voltaire, Franklin, Condorcet, Lalande, Dupaty, Elie de Beaumont, Antoine Court de Gebelin, Danton, Brissot, Camille Desmoulins, Sieyes, Bally, Romme, Garat, Pastoret, Jean-Reinhold Forster, Cabanis, Parny, Lacépède, Chamfort, François de Neufchâteau, Roucher, Jacques Delille, Florian, Guinguenée, Greuze, Charles Claude Vernet, Houdon, Jean-Michel Moreau, Joseph-Michel and Jacques Etienne Montgolfier. Concerning the work of this lodge, Findel writes: "There was no meeting which was not marked by a philosophical, historical, literary or artistic relationship; none where important charitable works were not collected."

The bar and the judiciary were represented with dignity in the French lodges of the 18th century. "Less numerous than the lawyers," writes Lois Amiable, "and less open to new ideas, the magistrates nevertheless provided an effective contribution: two of the key reforms that the Revolution had only time to draft, that of judicial investigation and that of penal law, were prepared by magistrates who were Freemasons." In 1789, the Venerables of five workshops in Paris and forty workshops in the provinces were magistrates. Portalis, Deseze, and Henrion de Pansey were Masons. All three had been honoured at the bar; Portalis became Minister of Worship in France; Deseze and Henrion de Pansey were the first presidents of the Court of Cassation during the Restoration.

We have just quoted Lois Amiable claiming, for magistrate Masons, the honour of having prepared the reform of judicial investigation and criminal law. In the long and hard struggle for the principles of justice and humanity, Jean-Baptiste Mercier Dupaty was of the highest order; he had been general lawyer, then *président à mortier* in the parliament of Bordeaux, but he renounced his office. With Élie de Beaumont, Legrand de Laleu, and Pastoret, all three lawyers in the Paris Parliament, and with Voltaire, and Condorcet, he defended the oppressed and, despite the relentless opposition of the supporters of the status quo, pursued citizen rehabilitation and the complete transformation of the judicial system and criminal laws. At that time, public opinion was fascinated by several resounding cases, such as the Calas and Sirven cases, and the case of the three men condemned to the Wheel, to mention only the principal trials in which unfair judgements were revised.

Already, in the Calas and Sirven affairs, the debate had taken on admirable proportions: criminal laws, the judicial system, and procedure had been examined and criticised; when, in 1786, Dupaty took up the defence of the three men condemned to the wheel, the whole old regime, one may say, was indicted.

On 11th August, 1785, the bailiwick of Clermont-Ferrand declared three guilty of night-time robberies involving violence and burglary; he condemned them to a lifetime on the galleys; on 20th October, the parliament of Paris condemned them to die on the Wheel, and Dupaty, Legrand de Laleu and Condorcet appealed to public opinion; the government was moved and an order from the king suspended the execution of the arrest. But parliament took revenge.

Dupaty's *Mémoire justificatif* [Supporting statement] and *Consultation* by Legrand de Laleu were condemned to be lacerated and burned by the executioner's hand, as attacks on the authority of parliament and consequently on the royal authority; the memoir was suppressed and Legrand de Laleu was suspended from the Order of Barristers for two years.

The times were no longer ripe for the courts to give precedence to their will; the King's Counsel seized upon the case of the three men sentenced to the wheel; he broke with procedure and, in Rouen, whereto the case was referred, Dupaty obtained a resounding triumph.

The abuse had manifested too clearly not to provoke a powerful movement: the exceptional courts, the extraordinary commissions, the secret procedures, torture, the odious penalties, the venality and heredity of the charges, the very basis of the right to punish; everything was examined and discussed. The government appointed a commission for the drafting of a new criminal code, it entrusted the presidency to Dupaty who chose, as collaborators, Legrand de Laleu and Pastoret. With the desire also to remedy immediately the most flagrant iniquities, by the edict of 1st May, 1788, he abolished the prior use of torture that intended to force the condemned to make additional confessions or to denounce their accomplices, much as he had abolished, on 24th December 1780, the preparatory questioning intended to extract confessions from the accused. It is true that, on 14th September, 1788, the disgrace of Chancellor Lamoignon resulted in the withdrawal of the 1st May edict and that it received no application.

Dupaty died on 17th September 1788; the final triumph came soon after: in 1789, 1790 and 1791, through several decrees, the National Assembly sought to found a new judicial order and, in the Constitution of 3rd September 1791, it proclaimed the fundamental principles of individual freedom and social justice.

CHAPTER IX

FREEMASONRY AND THE FRENCH REVOLUTION

I

THE QUESTION OF MASONRY'S INVOLVEMENT IN THE FRENCH Revolution was another subject of lively discussion.

Beginning in 1797, John Robison, the Scottish writer we have previously quoted, claimed to demonstrate the existence of a conspiracy of Freemasons and Illuminati against all religions and against all governments of Europe. He maintained that "the Mason Lodges in France were the hot-beds, where the seeds were soon, and tenderly reared, of all the pernicious doctrines which soon after choked every moral or religious cultivation." That same year, a French Jesuit, Augustin Barruel, published *Mémoires pour servir à l'Histoire du Jacobinisme* [Memoirs Illustrating the History of Jacobinism]. His exordium poses the thesis: "Towards the middle of the century in which we live," says the author, "three men met, all three penetrated with a deep hatred towards Christianity. These three men were Voltaire, D'Alembert and Frederic II, King of Prussia... To these three men a fourth must be added, Diderot." In the account of the infernal plot, Freemasonry was credited with the role of executor of decisions.

In 1811, the Count of Provence, the future Louis XVIII, twice denounced the Masons and Illuminati as the authors of the Revolution.

This was the theme favoured by reactionary writers. One, Jules de Polignac, the former minister to Charles X, developed the idea. He showed that 18th century philosophers were working to "overturn society" and relying on the Masonic lodges united with the Illuminati. "There is no doubt," he wrote, "that philosophers took advantage of the means of propaganda offered to them by a secret society spread over a large part of the globe, under the name of Freemasons, to achieve their goal." He depicted Weishaupt leaving the "philosophers" in charge of the destruction for which he advocated and dreaming above all of the means of seizing triumph on the day of victory. "He took the war name Spartacus," he added. "This nickname indicated his belief in the condition in which society found itself and revealed his intended purpose: it was necessary to free the people from the political and religious yoke, under which they groaned, and regenerate the dignity of free men that they had lost while they had been slaves. Such was, in fact, the great work to be carried out by the order of Illuminati, of which Weishaupt was the founder." Jules de Polignac described the propaganda work of the philosophers in all classes of society. "Soon," he said, "the philosophical sect could count several protective followers among its ranks; in addition to Frederick II, there were the Empress of Russia, Catherine II, Holy Roman Emperor, Joseph II, the Queen of Sweden and her son Prince Gustav, the King of Poland, the Landgraviate of Hesse-Kassel, the Duke of Brunswick, the Duke of Württemberg, Prince Louis of Württemberg, Charles Theodore, Prince-elector and Count Palatine, Princess Magdalena Augusta of Anhalt-Zerbst, and Wilhelm, Margrave of Brandenburg-Bayreuth. Eventually, in no doubt exaggerated joy, the patriarch of Ferney could write to one of his most ardent admirers: "There is not now a German prince who is not a philosopher, of the philosophy of incredulity."

When it comes to facts like those that came to pass at the end of the 18th century, one cannot speak of plot; the word does not reflect the grandiose reality: irreconcilable principles stood face to face; the struggle was inevitable with reason and freedom on one side, and religious fanaticism and political despotism on the other. But it is accurate to say that Masonry had a powerful contribution to the preparation of the formidable movement of 1789. Admittedly, a revolution does not explode on command; it is not enough to decree that an entire people rise up; however, it is impossible to deny the action of the lodges, the dissemination of information to which members devoted themselves, the part they took in dramatic events. An intelligible point of discussion arises: without Freemasonry, could France have freed itself and set a glorious example for the modern world? This question must be answered in the negative.

Louis Blanc points out that Freemasons were revolutionaries who were far more active than the Encyclopaedists. He insists on the effects that arose from the association between men of all ranks, men who considered themselves equal and who rejected hereditary pride and birth privileges. He argues that, despite all the reservations contained in the Masonic instructions concerning submission to the laws, the naturally revolutionary influences of Freemasonry had to prevail. "By the mere fact of the constitutive basis of its existence," he said, "Freemasonry tended to decry the institutions of the outside world that enveloped it." "Those who were part of it," he also said, "continued to be, in profane society, rich or poor, noble or plebeian; but within the lodges, temples that were open to the practice of a higher way of life, the rich, the poor, the noble, and the plebeian, had to recognise themselves as equal and call themselves brothers. It was an indirect, yet real and ongoing, denunciation of inequities, of the hardships of social order; it was propaganda in action, a living sermon." Henri Martin expresses the same thought. "Masonry," he wrote, "was the laboratory of Revolution."

One of the historians of Masonry, whom we have quoted several times already, protests against what he calls the reproach made to the institution "to have dominated and even executed the French Revolution". Certainly, let us repeat, it was not as a result of clear and formal resolutions voted in the lodges that the storm broke out; in this sense, Findel did deny the immediate and direct operation of Masonry on the events of the late 18th century..: but where the learned writer is mistaken is when he says that it is difficult to resolve the question of whether, by its humanitarian tendencies, by the unwavering sentiment of human dignity, by its principles of freedom, equality and fraternity, by its eminently free constitution, and in accordance with reason, Masonry promoted the improvement of the political situation, the progress in the direction of humanity and the demand of human rights.

As we have said, we must proclaim that without Masonry, the French Revolution could not have been accomplished. Indeed, public opinion had to be won over to new ideas and the programme of reformation required allegiance and support. This slow preliminary work was carried out by the lodges; thanks to them, across the territory meetings were held where progressive theories were exposed and acclaimed and where, more importantly than one may think, men gathered who were able to discuss and to vote. It was noted, in fact, that at the Convention, the deputies of the Third Estate had, over and above the representatives of the nobility and the clergy, the great advantage of being accustomed to the practices of deliberative assemblies. "For French Freemasonry of the 18th century," wrote Louis Amiable, "to have been able to play the role that prompted curses from the supporters of the old regime, it was necessary that, through the quality of its followers, it became the intellectual and moral elite of the nation; it was also necessary that the privileged classes were represented by the best of the men who composed them. If, in June 1789, the deputies of the clergy, then those of the nobility, joined the deputies of the Third Estate to form the National Assembly, it is to be believed that it was because a certain number of these ecclesiastics and these gentlemen had taken to the habit of deliberating with simple commoners in the lodges on a level of the most perfect equality and in the feelings of the most cordial brotherhood. If the destruction of feudal privileges was the work of those who benefitted from them, it is because the impetus was given by some of the ancient lords who had already renounced any superiority of rank among their brothers; and one can say that the renunciations of the night of 4th August, ordered by the principles that had been propagated by Freemasonry, were improvised only in appearance."

We have mentioned the names of some illustrious Masons who took part in the revolutionary drama; the publication of the lists of the people who composed the lodges towards the end of the 18th century would confirm what we have just said and would add many new names to those masons who are already known.

It would show that Louis Blanc was correct to write that most revolutionaries were affiliated with Freemasonry.

We saw that in 1787 there were 636 lodges under the direction of the two Masonic powers of France, the Grand Orient and the Grand Lodge of France; these lodges generally had many members; a historian, George Kloss, notes that, in France, the Masons were recruited from all classes of society; an enemy of the lodges, Augustin Barruel, calls the suburb Saint-Antoine and the suburb Saint-Marceau “Masonised”. Barruel estimates the number of French Masons at 600,000 at the time of the Revolution. “At least five hundred thousand,” he wrote, “scattered throughout all parts of France were ready to rise at the first signal of insurrection.” This is an obvious exaggeration; but historical scenes demonstrate the intervention of the lodges and conclude the existence of many members. One of these scenes took place on 17th July, 1789, when Louis XVI went to Paris City Hall. Louis Blanc recounts: “Instead of Grève, the King had to contemplate a strange ceremony. Most of the revolutionaries, as we have said, were affiliated with the secret societies of Freemasonry. Now, when a foreign brother presents himself as a visitor in a lodge, if he is honoured with a high rank, the members of the lodge line up on his way and, joining their swords above his head, they form what is called the Arch of Steel or Steel Vault. This singular honour was given to Louis XVI, at the moment when he set foot on the ground to climb the stairs of the town hall. With a firm step, he walked under this cradle of crossed blades and, to the sound of applause, entered the great hall.” In the events that took place in Paris, four characters played important roles. Jean Sylvain Bailly had just been proclaimed Mayor of Paris, and it was in this capacity that he welcomed the sovereign; La Fayette had been appointed by acclamation commander-in-chief of France’s National Guard; Adrien-Nicolas Piédefer, Marquis de La Salle, had been designated as second commander; Moreau de Saint-Méry, president of the assembly of the electors of Paris, lectured Louis XVI at length. All four were Masons.

II

THE INFLUENCE OF THE FRENCH LODGES WAS EXERCISED beyond the frontiers; already in 1797, this influence was, as we have seen, denounced by John Robison. Some lodges placed under the obedience of the Masonic powers of France occupied neighbouring countries; other lodges of these countries were in sustained correspondence with French lodges. This explains the welcome received by the men of the revolution when the work of liberation began outside France. In Mainz, for example, George Forster led the *Gesellschaft der Freunde der Freiheit und Gleichheit* [Society of the Friends of Liberty and Equality]; in Aix-la-Chapelle the society *Égalité, liberté et fraternité* had been formed; in Belgium and the United Provinces circles of propaganda had also been formed; thus, the *Société des Amis de la Liberté & de l'Égalité* was created in Brussels. All these associations were linked to Masonic workshops by the fact that their most active members were Masons.

When, even in France, the bloody struggles took place, the peace of the lodges was deeply disturbed. Illustrious brothers fell victim to political hatred; dissension broke out. On the very question of polity, there was a great deal of division. The lodges of the Scottish Rite were generally favourable to the monarchy: the Grand Lodge of France ceased its operations on 31st July, 1791; it even seems that in the lodges under its authority, the brothers who were entangled in the public affairs did not attend beyond 1790; they stated that they were defending a lost cause and, discouraged, they abandoned the fight. The Grand Orient held out longer. In 1791, it continued to install new lodges; it does not even seem to have ceased operations in 1793 and 1794; several members remained at their posts. However, in December 1792, the Duke of Orléans, who signed himself Louis Philippe Joseph Égalité, resigned as national

Grand Master. The resignation was accepted on 13th May, 1793, but the Grand Orient decided to postpone the new election. The Duke of Orléans made his resignation known through the press: "I entered Masonry, which is the very image of equality," he writes, "at a time when no one could have foreseen our revolution, just as I entered parliament, which is the very image of freedom. But I have since abandoned these ghosts for reality... Not knowing how the Grand Orient is composed and believing, moreover, that a republic must, especially at the beginning of its institution, tolerate no mystery, and no secret assembly, I no longer wish to interfere with what concerns either the Grand Orient or the Freemason assemblies." On 24th November, 1793, the Grand Orient published a circular concerning administrative matters.

In the midst of the turmoil, lodges were still active; it seems that this was the case for some military lodges; it was also the case for three Paris workshops: the *Guillaume Tell* lodge which took, in 1793, the name *Le centre des amis* [Centre of Friends]; the *Les amis de la liberté* [Friends of Freedom] lodge and the *Saint-Louis de Martinique* lodge.

"These three lodges," Findel said, "maintained the sacred fire, for they worked on without interruption or fear. When the two latter were questioned, concerning the existence of the Grand Orient, they did not reply, for, though the Lodges were composed of members who had belonged to the Grand Orient, the Brethren did not consider themselves authorised to answer in its name, and this silence led to the conclusion that that authority had ceased to exist; however, no new Grand Orient was established, and it was determined to continue to work in silence. It was not until 1793 that Alexandre Roettiers de Montaleau would invite his brothers to create a new Masonic centre."

The reconstitution of the Grand Orient took place on 27th December, 1795. Work resumed in the Grand Lodge of France in October 1796. Almost immediately sixteen lodges dependent on the Grand Orient were in operation; in 1800, there were seventy-four; in 1802, the number increased to one hundred and fourteen, and in 1804, it exceeded three hundred. The Grand Lodge of France also had a large number of lodges. On 3rd December, 1804, an arrangement was signed between the two Masonic powers in order to avoid future dissent between the Masons of the two rites; it is true that only a few years later, it was denounced.

The First French Empire was a period of true prosperity for Freemasonry. The Grand Orient ended up with 826 lodges and 337 chapters in its dominion, and the names of those who composed it show very well the importance that the institution had acquired. In 1807, to cite only this year, Joseph-Napoléon Bonaparte, King of Naples and Sicily, Grand Elector of France, was Grand Master; Jean Jacques Régis de Cambacérès, Prince of the Empire, and Joachim-Napoléon Murat, the first Prince of Murat, were assistant Grand Masters; among the great dignitaries were marshals Kellermann, Masséna, Lannes, Angereau, Lefebvre, Serrurier, Brune, Mortier, Soult, councillor of state Joseph Jérôme Siméon, Minister of Police Joseph Fouché, the Minister of Justice Régnier, Attorney General at the Court of Cassation Philippe-Antoine Merlin de Douai, and illustrious scholars like Lalande and Lacépède.

III

To the developments concerning the part played by Masonry in the Revolution of 1789, it may be interesting to add some information relating to the Revolution of 1830 and the Revolution of 1848.

With the days of July 1830 scarcely elapsed, Masons wanted to hold a festival of the freedom in Paris; three lodges met for this purpose on 6th August, 1830; Dupin the Younger presided; successively, the speakers celebrated the great political event which had just occurred. On 10th October, Scottish Masonry organised a banquet which was attended by the Masons who had been wounded during the fights against the soldiers of Charles X. The Duke of Choiseul-Praslin occupied the presidency. The hero of the festival was La Fayette who, at the beginning of the revolutionary movement, had been acclaimed commander-in-chief of the National Guard of France, and who had presented Louis Philippe to the people, defining the new regime: a popular throne surrounded by republican institutions; La Fayette was then 73 years old. At the age of 20, he had left for the United States where he shed his blood for the cause of independence; a few years later, he played an important role in the Assembly of Notables, the Estates General and the National Constituent Assembly; in 1792, he commanded the army which fought against the Austrians; taken prisoner by them, he suffered long years of captivity. The orator, Pierre Berville, recalled these glorious services in a speech in which he stated that the triumph of freedom and equality had restored to France its rights and its power. On 16th October, 1830, Masons organised a feast at the City Hall in Paris; five hundred brothers attended; one of the speakers recalled how the people had broken a ministry which "was the enemy of liberal institutions and which relied on a prince who had sworn their overthrow".

In 1848, Masonry also showed its animated feelings with regard to the Revolution.

Findel tells the story while expressing his disapproval. "On 4th March, 1848," he wrote, "In consequence of an invitation from Brother Bertrand, who had been chosen as Grand Master Delegate in 1847, the Grand Orient of France held a celebration in commemoration of those who had fallen in the February struggle. It was likewise determined in this assembly that a subscription should be opened for the better relief of those who had been wounded in the struggle. The list was immediately headed by a contribution of 500 francs, and it was voted that an address, in the name of the French Freemasons, should be presented to the Provisional Government. On 6th March, a committee, composed of six of the highest officials, was elected to deliver this address. Brothers Crémieux, Garnier-Pagès, Marrast, and Pagnierre received the deputation, dressed in Masonic attire. "Although the French Masonic fraternity," it says in the address, which was appropriately answered by Crémieux, "has in accordance to its statutes kept itself aloof from all political questions, it cannot withhold the expression of its feelings at the grand national and social movement which has just taken place. On the banners of the Freemasons have at all times been displayed the words "Liberty, Equality, and Fraternity", and when they decry these same words, borne on the standard of the French nation, they joyfully welcome in them the triumph of their principles, and consider themselves fortunate in being able to cry out, that the whole of their native land has through them received Masonic consecration."

A few years later, an illustrious Mason, Pierre-Theodore Verhaegen, examined the question of whether Masonry could refrain longer from dealing with major political issues and whether the defence of dealing with religion and politics during its operations, which is found in the rules of the

Grand Lodge and not in the General Statutes, could not be annihilated by another decision of the Grand Lodge.

It was at the Solstitial Festival celebrated by the Grand Orient of Belgium, on 24th June, 1854. Verhaegen was the interim Grand Master. He said that Masonry had something to do with the political situation. "It cannot be without purpose and without fruitfulness," he said, "that intelligent, good patriots, friends of progress and freedom, come together in so many parts of the country. The Masonic associations would be greatly at fault if they confined themselves to sterile labour, while on all sides the enemy organised itself, while the tenebrous league of ignorance and oppression stretched its traps in the shadows and increased, through fear and egotism, its fatal power which constantly grows. I know that, by setting foot on this ground, I will arouse apprehensions and scruples in any timorous souls. One may say that this is a steep and dangerous slope for Masonry, that our statutes forbid any political or religious discussion. This must, once and for all, be seriously examined; Masonry must finally say what it thinks and what it wants about this strange choice between keeping quiet or violating its own laws. First, let us note that, in many circumstances, Masonry has unanimously ignored this restriction. It was actively involved in political struggles, and when the triumph of its cause, greeted by the entire nation, showed how sympathetic it was to the country, who would dare to blame it? That would be to slander history, to deny the immense service rendered to the country. When I question our institution's past, do I not see that Masonry has always been the vigilant eye that watches over the march of the political vessel? Is it not Masonry that lights, in the darkness of the temple, the beacon of light that signals the pitfalls, that sounds the cry of alarm in times of danger? Does history not answer as it unfolds? Whenever necessary, did not Masonry form the centre, the support point of resistance to the encroachment of error and lies, on whatever side they came? And with regards to what it has already done, can it no longer know and do thus under such circumstances?"

CHAPTER X

FREEMASONRY AND MODERN SOCIETY

I

On the first pages of this book, we listed some of the areas in which Masonry exerted influence; we may summarise its work by saying that it had the largest impact on the formation of modern society.

We know what characterises the modern organisation of the State: it is secularisation, i.e. the negation of any religious authority in the political and civil domain; it is also the establishment of security, it is national sovereignty, the separation of powers, with legislative power entrusted to the chambers, the individual rights of equality and security, the right to communicate thought, freedom in matters of worship. In the elaboration of this regime, the lodge members were no doubt not alone in bringing their zeal and pooling their efforts, but we must do them justice by saying that, everywhere, they were among the most devoted and zealous supporters of the new order of things.

Likewise, Masonry cannot claim the glory of having first proclaimed "liberty, equality, fraternity", but it can take pride in the fact that its most famous followers have eloquently expounded on these principles and have succeeded above all others in having them adopted. They are glorious names in the history of tolerance and freedom, such as Montesquieu, Voltaire and Lessing, and next to these names, how many other illustrious names could Masonry not register, if the lists of its lodges were published? Will we ever understand the great influence that the compact mass of Masons had on the course of events? That is to say, the so many thousands of men, independent by character, by education, by situation, all animated by will and energy? Without doubt, there are countries where the political action of the lodges was erased; when freedom reigns, one should not arm oneself to conquer it. But even in these fortunate countries, Masonry exerted influence by striving above all to make religious peace reign. We too often forget the services to the emancipation of the Catholics of Great Britain rendered by an eminent Mason, George Canning, who died almost on the eve of triumph.

II

IN THE DOMAIN OF IDEOLOGY, THERE IS ONE NOTION THAT Masonry has always preached: the idea of progress.

Most probably, it was introduced into all Masonic doctrines by the Rose Cross which, as we have said, appeared at the beginning of the 18th century, and which many followers entered. The perfectibility of man was, together with the belief in a divine spirit spread across the universe, a fundamental theory of the movement. The Belgian Jean-Baptiste Van Helmont had preached the doctrine of perfectibility in all domains, and, as far as the religious field was concerned, he predicted that 1st January, 1700, would see the coming of a new religion, the Philadelphians, that is to say brotherly love.

Among the eminent Masons dedicated to the idea of progress are Voltaire, Lessing and Condorcet. It is Condorcet who gives us these powerful words: "Is it not a term in which the natural limits of our spirit would make all progress impossible? No, as enlightenment increases, as methods of learning are perfected, the human spirit seems to enlarge and limits to retreat... What is the object of the improvement of laws and public institutions, consequent upon the progress of these sciences, but to reconcile, to approximate, to blend and unite into one mass the common interest of each individual with the common interest of all?"

III

WE MAKE INTERESTING FINDINGS WHEN WE EXAMINE THE development of the principles on which modern society is based and when we study the institutions that serve to ensure the application of these principles. Not only does it appear that these principles and institutions are in conformity with Masonry's teachings, but it has been proven that often it was Masons who merited being accepted in the fundamental charters of the modern States.

The name Montesquieu must always be cited when it comes to political law and *De l'esprit de lois* [The Spirit of the Laws] is, even today, an abundant source. "The human race," Condorcet was able to say, "had lost its way; Montesquieu found it and returned them to it." The merit goes to Montesquieu for having ensured the triumph of the principle of the separation of powers, which secures any liberal regime; one detail is significant; reactionary writers reproached him as proof of hostility towards the monarchy; ignorant that he was a Mason, they argued that he was the intimate friend of a lodge Venerable, Helvétius; this was, in their opinion, connected with "the vast conspiracy" organised by the lodges!

The "declarations of human and civil rights" which are at the head of several modern constitutions, are of Masonic origin; they first appeared in the English colonies of North America where they shook off the yoke of the metropolis. In France, Masons highlighted the usefulness of asserting citizens' rights and liberties. Brissot, a Mason, expressed himself on this subject in the writing he published in 1789, under the title *Plan de Conduite pour les Députés du peuple aux États-Généraux* [Plan of Conduct for the Deputies of the People of the States-General]. On 11th July, 1789, La Fayette, a Mason, exposed the broad outlines of a project he had directed to the National Assembly. First of all, he introduced the two useful purposes of a declaration. It was to recall the feelings that nature has engraved in the heart of every individual; it was also to express the "eternal truths from which all institutions must stem" and to become the guide that leads the representatives of a nation back to the source of natural law. "For a nation to love freedom," he said, "it is enough for it to be known, and for it to be free, for it to be desired." In the projects he had prepared, La Fayette affirmed the principle of the separation of powers and the maxim that all sovereignty derives from the nation; he proclaimed that nature had made men free and equal; he said that man is born with inalienable rights; the freedom of his opinions, the care of his honour and life, the right of property, the entire disposition of his person, his industry and all his favours, the communication of his thoughts by all possible means, the search for well-being and resistance to oppression.

The question of knowing whether a declaration of human and citizens' rights should be at the head of the constitution was discussed in sessions on 1st, 2nd and 3rd August, 1789; it was resolved affirmatively; from 18th to 27th August, 1789, the content of a declaration was examined and voted on: it comprises seventeen articles and forms the preamble to the constitution of 3rd September 1791.

Condorcet also endeavoured to demonstrate the importance of a declaration: he wanted such a document to be voted on before any other provision by an assembly called upon to draft a constitution; it was, in his opinion, the only way to prevent tyranny "because that is, in essence, the violation of human rights."

Another Mason, Jean-Sylvain Bailly, wrote in his *Mémoires*: "If human rights had not been forgotten or ignored, there would not have been a revolution; the first task of this revolution had to be the declaration of rights: it is the act of taking possession of freedom, an act performed by us, but which belongs to all humanity as it belongs to us."

An eminent jurisconsult, Esmein, the author of *Élements de Droit Constitutionnel* [Elements of Constitutional Law] characterises the *Déclarations des droits de l'homme et du citoyen* [The Declaration of the Rights of Man and of the Citizen]. "They are," he says, "a direct product of 18th century philosophy and the movement of spirit it developed. These are the main axioms of philosophers and publicists, as well as the foundations of a just and rational political organisation, which the authors of the new constitutions solemnly proclaimed would be applied. Declarations of rights emanate from bodies possessing legal and even sovereign authority, from constituent assemblies; but they are not precise and enforceable articles of law. They are, purely and simply, declarations of principles, and until now we have never seen anything like them."

This description and appreciation are complete if we add that, in the actualisation of the idea, Masonry was preponderant and that various articles in the declarations were much the same as Masonic maxims and precepts.

From this point of view, some passages are instructive. "The National Assembly," it reads, "therefore recognises and declares, in the presence and under the auspices of the Supreme Being, the following rights of man and citizen:

Article First - Men are born and remain free and equal in rights. Social distinctions may be based only on considerations of the common good.

Article 2 - The aim of every political association is the preservation of the natural and imprescriptible rights of man. These rights are Liberty, Property, Safety and Resistance to Oppression."

"The Law," says Article 6, "is the expression of the general will. All citizens have the right to take part, personally or through their representatives, in its making. It must be the same for all, whether it protects or punishes."

Article 10 states: "No one may be disturbed on account of his opinions, even religious ones, as long as the manifestation of such opinions does not interfere with the established Law and Order."

"The free communication of ideas and of opinions," said in Article 11, "is one of the most precious rights of man. Any citizen may therefore speak, write and publish freely, except what is tantamount to the abuse of this liberty in the cases determined by Law."

These were all affirmations of the Masonic motto: "Liberty, equality, fraternity."

IV

Some quotations will help to better understand the doctrines of Masonry.

As we have seen, many of these doctrines are related to early 18th century English deism; they are therefore in opposition to any positive religion; they deny the legitimacy of any priesthood or hierarchy.

In 1712, Anthony Collins, in his *A Discourse Of Free Thinking: Occasioned By The Rise And Growth Of A Sect Called Free Thinkers*, based the right to think freely on man's duty to know the truth. "What other way," he asks, "may one discover the truth than through *Free-Thinking*?" He made free thought a duty, because without it men cannot perfect themselves.

In 1720, in *Pantheisticon*, which must be a portrait of Masonic lodges, John Toland wrote: "To live happily, virtue alone is enough; it is its own reward."[6]

Note that Toland is a pantheist. The Socratica, whose dialogues and songs were reproduced in *Pantheisticon*, affirms its belief in "a God who is all in all, eternal and immense, who has not been born and who will not die; in whom men live, move and exist."[7]

---

6 Ad beate vivendum sola sufficit Virtus,
suaque sibi est satis ampla merces.

7 In Mundo omnia sunt Unum,
Unumque est Omne in omnibus,
... Quod Omne in omnibus, Deus est,
Aeternus ac immensus,
Neque genitus neque interiturus.
In eo vivimus, movemur, et existimus,

It celebrates the joy of living; it glorifies nature, it proclaims that contemplation of natural things is the most useful of the sciences; it teaches that man must feel the cost of life and at the same time not fear death.[8]

In the appendix to *Pantheisticon*, Toland recalled that the princes and politicians, enemies of superstition, owed this to the fact that his era possessed religious liberty for the greater benefit of literature, of commerce between men, and of concord between citizens. He wanted to realise the reign of reason. *Ratio est vera et prima lex ; lux lumenque vitae:* "reason is the true and first law; it is the light and clarity of life". *Vera lex, recta ratio*; "Right reason is the true law". *Nullius in verba jurandum, nedum in ipsius Socratis and hierotechnen execramur* ; "one must not swear on the word of anyone, not even on that of Socrates; let us curse all priestly science". These are all passages from dialogues between the president and the members of Socratica.

Lessing, a Mason, wrote these lines: "It is not the truth that a man possesses or believes he possesses that determines the value of this man, it is the loyal work that he does to achieve it; for it is not by possession but by the pursuit of truth that strength increases; possession makes one indolent, lazy, proud."

8 Natura rerum ut jucunda contemplatio,
Sic est utilissima scientia...
..... Ut sit mens sana in corpore sano
Usque optandum est :
Ac ut Vita non leviter deserenda,
Sic nunquam timenda Mors est.
..... Lætitia liberi est, tristitia servi indicium.
..... Rerum scrutamur causas
Ut vitam hilare,
Ut mortem tranquille obeamus.

Helvétius, Venerable of the lodge *Les sciences*, wrote: "No one has a right to the air I breathe, nor to the noblest function of my mind, above that which I judge for myself."

Jurisconsults deifying the laws came to teach that they were sacrosanct deep within their conscience; in other words, the Christian who does not observe these laws sins against the will of his God. Toland indicated the real reason for submission to the laws: one must respect them because without them nothing is clean, nothing is safe; one must be a slave to be free.[9] A little-known maxim of Montesquieu's reads thus: "A thing is not just because it is law, but it must be law because it is just."

Tolerance within Freemasonry had to overcome the prejudices which, for centuries, had aroused Christians' hatred and anger towards Jews. We saw that in 1746 and 1747, the lodge *L'anglais* [The English] of Bordeaux decided that only Christians could be initiated. In 1785, Adolphe de Knigge, a Freemason and member of the Illuminati, taught that the Mason must consider the follower of any religion, the Jew, the Muslim, the Pagan, as his neighbour; he must see in them men like him, worthy of respect, love and assistance; but he added that none other than Christians, no matter of what sect, may be welcomed into the order. The narrowness of these views was in contradiction with the very essence of Masonic doctrine. We may note that already in the 18th century, Jews were members of lodges, as were Muslims. In the 19th century, in the very heart of Masonry, there were protests against the workshops that excluded Israelites. Thus, in 1845, the Count of Zetland asked to put the matter before the Grand Lodge of England; as

---

9 At legibus parere necesse est,
Nam sine bis nil proprium.
Legum idcirco servi sumus
Ut liberi esse possimus.

the Grand Lodge of Berlin, the *Royal York zur Freundschaft* [Royal York of Friendship], had refused to admit Jewish brothers as visitors who were carrying diplomas delivered by English lodges, he raised a protest against this procedure and demanded an explanation. Some twenty years later, German Masonry took care of the admissibility of non-Christians. "The exchange of opinions which took place on this subject," writes Findel, "although the necessary moderation and circumspection was not always observed, was beneficial in that it brought the matter to light and made an important step towards a solution: several large German lodges, such as *Eklektische Bund* [Eclectic Union], the Grand Lodge of Frankfurt, and the Grand Lodge *Zur Sonne* [To the Sun] of Bayreuth returned to the former principles of Freemasonry which did not permit the admission of non-Christians. The Grand National Mother Lodge *Zu den drei Weltkugeln* [The Three Globes] and the *Royal York zur Freundschaft* of Berlin warned the lodges in their dominion to take into account in future no more than the attestations of good conduct issued to the brothers by the lodges, without inquiring into their worship."

In 1869, the congress of the Eastern lodges was addressed with a proposal aiming to suppress the provision in the statutes of the Grand Orient which affirmed, as a foundation of the Masonic order, the existence of God and the immortality of the soul.

On 14th September 1877, at the Grand Convent in Paris, the provision was abolished and replaced by a new text. "Freemasonry," it reads, "has as its principles: absolute freedom of conscience and human solidarity.

It does not exclude anyone for their beliefs. Its motto is: Liberty, equality, fraternity."

Masonry also adjudicated on the admission of neophytes belonging to races other than the white race.

We mentioned that a black lodge, *African lodge*, was created in 1775. In the last half of the 19th century, several Masonic bodies delivered their views categorically. Let us quote the declaration made on 8th July, 1869, by the Grand Orient of France. "The Masons under the obedience of the Grand Orient of France," it says, "represented by their legal representatives in the convent of 5869, affirm that mankind and Masonry are outraged when colour, race or religion is sufficient to prohibit a layman from being in the Masonic family." The declaration was brought to the knowledge of all Masonic powers across the globe, and it was resolved to break any alliance with those who would not adhere to it. Let us also quote the decision taken, on 8th June, 1873, in the regimen of the great confederate lodges of Germany, held in Bayreuth under the presidency of Bluntschli. It was solemnly proclaimed that difference of race and colour should not constitute an obstacle to initiation.

In the history of the struggle against intolerance, it is not without interest to quote the circular sent in 1865 by the lodge *Ruprecht zu den fünf Rosen* [Ruprecht to the five Roses] of Heidelberg to the lodges in its correspondence and the circular sent, in 1860, to the Masonic powers of the whole world by the Grand Lodge *Zur Sonne* of Bayreuth. Both are the work of Bluntschli; they were written, the first on the occasion of an address given by Pope Pius IX, the second on the occasion of the oecumenical council of the Vatican. With eloquence, they show papacy as the enemy of modern Masonry and civilisation, papacy that condemns all liberties, which are the indispensable security of the fabric of society, and curses all philosophy and science that do not bow down before their hierarchy.

From 1724, Lord Dalkeith had the Grand Lodge of London adopt a proposal for the creation of a charitable fund, the Fund of Benevolence. Since then, the lodges have taken on many charitable initiatives in different countries: care of the sick, relief to orphans, education. In his excellent work, *Les Francs-Maçons*, Pierre Tempels notes that the followers of Masonry have never ceased to attach the greatest importance to the philanthropic dimension of their institution: "Every lodge," he says, "has a charitable fund financed by compulsory contributions. The statutes prescribe assistance to widows and orphans, to unhappy brothers, to travellers in distress."

It is impossible to make a detailed enumeration of all the Masonic foundations. But it would be ungrateful, as a Belgian, not to recall that the Free University of Brussels was created by the lodges. "The liberal party created the University of Brussels," says Léon Vanderkindere. "Beginning in 1831, some men devoted to the cause of progress had dreamed of this grandiose but difficult project; one had hesitated however, one had waited. By 1834, hesitation was no longer permitted. And yet the venture seemed foolhardy. To oppose the reunited forces of the Church, its inexhaustible resources, the efforts of a small number of citizens left to themselves, was to attempt an undertaking the outcome of which could not be completely assured. Pierre-Théodore Verhaegen is graced with the honour of daring to face peril, of not doubting success, of communicating his belief to others, of bringing the task to a successful conclusion. In June 1834, on the day of the summer solstice festival, at *Les amis philanthropes* in Brussels, he exhibited his project in the presence of numerous Masons from various parts of Belgium and was able to win over his audience. Beyond Freemasonry the idea gained publicity; it made rapid progress in public opinion. Everyone understood that the liberal party, that freedom itself, would be eternally jeopardised if bishops were left to be masters of instruction."

To the notion of equality, a notion inseparable from human dignity, the lodges provided considerable support; it is thanks to them, we may say, that it triumphed towards the end of the 18th century, in countries such as the United States first, then France. John Toland's *Pantheisticon* contained the clearest statements: "Let us be called equal and brothers," said the president of the Socratica. "Let us be called colleagues and friends", replied the members.[10] *Aequales praestantissimi*, "very excellent and equal", the president also said.

By its very essence, Masonry must want to achieve equality; in fact, when one examines the composition of the congresses and the constituents which, in different countries, inscribed this principle into charters and laws, one notices that these assemblies counted many Masons among their members. In 18th century France, fighting against despotism, the thesis of natural equality was exhibited in Volume V of Diderot and d'Alembert's *Encyclopédie,* published in 1755. "Natural equality," wrote the knight of Jaucourt, "is the principle and foundation of freedom." It was on the principle of this equality that, with Anglican theologian Richard Hooker, Jaucourt founded all the duties of charity, humanity and justice to which men are obliged, one to another.

In the booklets which the electors handed over to their deputies at the Estates General of 1789, and which, in general, were drafted under the inspiration of the lodges, one article was proclaimed "the fundamental article of any constitution"; it was the article which stated: "All men are equal before their

---

10 Aequales vocemur et fratres,
Sodales item atque amici.

civil association; in any political society, they must all be equal in rights."

We have reproduced the text of the First Article of the 1789 Declaration of Human Rights.

On the topic of public law, one may mention the speech delivered in 1844 by Johann Kaspar Bluntschli at the founding of the Union of Swiss Lodges; it deals with the situation of Masonry before the State and the Churches.

The speaker, who at that time was a professor at the University of Zurich, asked the question: "Would Masonry have a clean future without the State, without the Church, or alongside the State and the Church? Does it truly have a principle on life which is its own, belonging neither to the State nor to the Church, which can be neither recognised nor fully developed?" Bluntschli meant by the Church the religious community of men, as he meant by the State their political community. To the question he asked, he responded in the negative. "The State and the Church, in their highest sense," he said, "understand all human life; without them, there is no place left for another community of men." This was the solution he pronounced when the Church and the State fulfilled the mission he assigned them. But he was aware of the truth. "The State and the Church at present," he added, "are not always aware of their principle on life; often they ignore it, deny it, harm it. Had the principle of humanity once completely penetrated the State and the Church, it would be recognised and actualised by them in general, and Masonry would have ceased to exist. But as long as State and Church have not become completely human, so long Masonry has within "humanity" a principle that it can claim relatively as its own, as long as it has the right to exist." Bluntschli determined the sphere of action. "Where the spirit of persecution and the accusations of heresy begin to show themselves in the churches, there begins the task of Masonry and its duty to enter into the competition on the side of humanity, which takes various directions and various forms."

CHAPTER XI

FREEMASONRY AND INTERNATIONAL LAW

I

MASONRY HAS AIDED THE DISSEMINATION OF INTERNATIONAL law. Masons have sought to highlight the points of contact it has had with this aspect of political science. "If the ideas and principles of Freemasonry are true," wrote Joseph Schauberg in 1861, "they must be found in the everyday existence of men and peoples and in there must lie their history; indeed, at the foundation of humanity one must find the same laws as at the foundation of the world of nature and at the foundation of the universe. The life of man and the life of men, that is, the life of humanity and the life of peoples and States, have only one purpose, one law, although this law may seem diverse... The laws, according to which peoples and States act towards each other, are called the rights of man and, in essence, the history of the rights of man must coincide with the history of Freemasonry: the rights of man and Freemasonry have the same history." In developing this thought, the author said that, in antiquity, the rights of man and Masonry were not known, but that partial applications of them occurred, since hospitality and respect for the lives of defeated enemies were permitted in the relations between populations, and there were secret doctrines and philosophical teachings through which, after a time, Freemasonry was formed. He added that in the Middle Ages Christianity was intolerant towards other religions and to Christians who had fallen into heresy, and granted the peace of God only to Catholics. Finally, he mentioned the progress being made in the transition from what he called the right of ecclesiastical people to the right of new people.

Findel displays similar considerations. "The fundamental thought and the main symbols of Freemasonry," he says, "go beyond the individual and embrace the whole of humanity; thus relationships are born between it and the right of people." He lists the characteristics of this right which is free from religious prejudice, rests on a purely human basis and promotes the development of nations. Findel even proposed the periodic meeting of a Masonic committee devoted to the advancement of national law and composed of national Grand Masters and nine jurisconsults.

II

THE NOTION OF PERPETUAL PEACE HAS BEEN ADOPTED BY MANY Masons and, in all cases, war is viewed with disfavour by Masonry. The 1723 *Constitutions* argue that "Masonry has always been outraged by war, murder, and disorder." We have seen the influence that the lodges had on the very constitution of the United States. It was an American Mason, Benjamin Franklin, who said: "When will humanity be convinced that all wars are very costly and harmful follies, and when will it decide to settle its disputes by arbitration?" When, on 31st May 1872, the United States Senate passed an important motion concerning the substitution of arbitration for peace, it honoured Franklin by reproducing his own words in the text.

In Franklin's *Memoirs and writings*, some generous pages feature. "By the original law of nations," he writes, "war and extirpation was the punishment of injury. Humanising by degrees, it admitted slavery instead of death. A farther step was the exchange of prisoners instead of slavery. Another, to respect more the property of private persons under conquest, and to be content with acquired dominion. Why should not the law of nations go on improving? Ages have intervened between its several steps; but, as knowledge of late increases rapidly, why should not those steps be quickened? Why should it not be agreed to as the future law of nations, that in any war hereafter the following descriptions of men should be undisturbed, have the protection of both sides, and be permitted to follow their employments in surety." Franklin mentioned farmers, fishermen, merchants and traffickers in unarmed ships; craftsmen and workers living in open cities; he demanded that enemy hospitals be respected. He said that it was in humanity's own interest that opportunities and motives for war should be diminished, and he saw the abolition of pillage and the eradication of war incentives as a means of achieving lasting peace. In 1783, Franklin proposed that the English government insert into the peace treaty an article containing the reforms which we have just mentioned; he did not succeed; but almost all these same reforms appeared, at the same time as other reforms, in the treaty which was concluded, on 10th September, 1785, between the United States and Prussia. Benjamin Franklin, Thomas Jefferson and John Adams, three Masons, signed as commissioners of the young republic; the King of Prussia was brother Frederick II.

In 1793, Washington, President of the United States, and Thomas Jefferson, Secretary of State, formulated the law of neutrality with admirable instructions. A competent jurisconsult, Richard Kleen, judges them in these terms: "These instructions of 1793, which were subsequently regularly applied and observed by the Washington cabinets, formed the most accomplished law of neutrality at the time of their publication. They are well ahead of their time and express our ideas... These principles, so favourable to an equitable regulation of neutral laws... have been spread not only by means of the domestic legislation of the United States, as well as by the dispatches and notes exchanged with foreign cabinets, but they have also been transformed into positive international law, by their insertion into numerous treaties with other powers. So, they were not long in being adopted, even outside the United States."

III

THE LODGES OFTEN SHOWED THEIR LOVE OF PEACE. IT IS A document little known in the secular world and which honours Belgian Masonry.

During the Franco-German war, the lodge *Les amis philanthropes*, established in Brussels, decided to send an address to all Masons in France and Germany. The address is dated 17th September, 1870. "All humanity is at stake," it reads. "The whole of Europe cannot think without blushing that after centuries of civilisation, after long practice of the rule of law, the people accustomed to entrusting to them the slightest differences in justice, reject all arbitration, and place the greatest stock in blind force... Isn't the 19th century civilised enough to live in peace? Masonry cannot leave this awful doubt unanswered. Placed above all distinctions of party, nation or race, political form or religious sect, Masonry wants to unite men by a bond that knows no borders; it can aspire to a moral power that is lacking in those who divide them. Our principles, which are contained in this old Masonic motto:

liberty, equality, fraternity, can be summarised in one word: justice."

In the great movement that in recent years has taken place throughout the world in favour of arbitration as a means of settling disputes between States, almost all the world's lodges have contributed their support. One such event occurred at the 1902 International Masonic Congress in Geneva. In solemn dress, the great orator of the *Alpina* Lodge, Eugène Borel, made a moving appeal to the brotherhood. On behalf of the delegates of the Grand Orient of France, a Mason recalled that in a plenary meeting of French lodges organised, in 1900, by the *Cosmos* lodge, a German brother expressed the wish that one day in the year be devoted to the celebration of the great notion of peace and arbitration between nations. A proposal along the same lines was tabled and the Convention passed the following motion: "The Congress expresses the wish that, throughout the universe, on 18th May, the anniversary of the opening of the Hague Conference, the Masonic workshops in each Orient, will gather in plenary and collective attire, celebrate the ideal of Peace and Justice among nations, one of the goals universal to Freemasonry, and instruct the International Bureau of Masonic Relations to transmit this wish to all the universal powers of Masonry." The motion was adopted; the communication was made and, consequently, the festival of peace is celebrated annually.

IV

WE HAVE SHOWN HOW THE MILITARY LODGES WERE ORGANISED. It is of little use, one may think, to insist on the happy effects that similar lodges exerted on the feelings that animated the fighters: they fulfilled their duty to their homeland, but they did not forget that humanity lay beyond the homeland and that they had to fulfil obligations towards their enemies.

"One of the noblest prerogatives of man," read the address of the lodge *Les amis philanthropes* from Brussels, "is to dedicate their lives to justice, to fill the earth with their corpses, with thousands of corpses, rather than to drag behind him an oppressed character, a wretched conscience... But this heroism of the resistance implies the crime of attack."

When war broke out, the lodges tried to soften its evils. In neutral countries, as in belligerent states, subscriptions and donations were collected, ambulances and hospitals were organised. The Franco-German War of 1870 gave rise to numerous acts of charity.

In the development of human rights, real progress was made when the distinction between Christian and non-Christian states practically disappeared. It should be noted that the government of the United States, under Masonic influence, has categorically declared itself on this subject. On 4th November, 1796, the Bey of Tripoli concluded in an agreement guaranteed by the dey of Algiers, 3rd January, 1797; it stipulated peace and friendship between the United States and Tripoli. It was stated in Article XI, "As the government of the United States of America is not in any sense founded on the Christian Religion, as it has in itself no character of enmity against the laws, religion or tranquility of Muslims, and as the said States never have entered into any war or act of hostility against any Mahomitan nation, it is declared by the parties that no pretext arising from religious opinions shall ever produce an interruption of the harmony existing between the two countries." It is not without use to cite Article XII. "In case of any dispute arising from a notation of any of the articles of this treaty no appeal shall be made to arms, nor shall war be declared on any pretext whatever. But if the Consul residing at the place where the dispute shall happen shall not be able to settle the same, an amicable reference shall be made to the mutual friend of the parties, the Dey of Algiers, the parties hereby engaging to abide by his decision."

V

THE POLITICAL PROBLEM OF LEGITIMACY AROSE BEFORE ENGLISH Masonry at the beginning of the 18th century: it was a question of whether some divine right made dynasties somehow exceptional, or whether the will of the nation should be listened to. The lodges of London, which constituted a Grand Lodge in 1717, had not hesitated; they declared themselves against the claims of the Stuarts; it must even be noted that the *Constitutions* written by James Anderson gave Masons the duty to be a pagan subject of the country where he lived and worked, and that, adding precision to the thought, they added that loyal brotherhood could not provide cover to the "government for the time being". One of the English deists whose philosophical views had a considerable influence on Freemasonry had already dealt with the question of the rights of the *de facto* sovereign and the rights of the *de jure* sovereign. That was Matthew Tindal. Shortly after the accession of William III and Mary II, King James II, exiled in France, who claimed to be the legitimate king, issued letters of marque and commissioned privateers to wage war against William and the English under his government. The English Privy Council addressed members of the College of Lawyers; two of them declared the letters of marque illegal: it was Littleton and Tindal. The latter collected the evidence which related to his arguments into a brochure published in London in 1694.

Never, it must be said in its honour, did Masonry consider it a duty to obey the will of an oppressive and tyrannical government.

A lover of freedom, it was demanded in all periods of its life and in all spheres of human activity; Masonry wanted to achieve freedom in the political realm. We have mentioned the ardour that its members displayed in the XVIII century; without going into greater details that would oblige us to summarise the history of almost all countries, we can recall the help provided by the lodges to the liberation of Greece and to the renovation of Italy.

In 1829, a Masonic brochure celebrated the assistance that the members of the order had given to the Greek populations, insurgent against the Turkish oppression. "The Greeks," he said, "were asking for life, laws, morals, freedom and peace from the universe. Who made the first cries of shame, pity and mercy? Aren't they Masons?" The brochure invoked the reception given, on 30th August, 1824, to the deputies of the lodge *L'Espérance*, of Brussels, by the lodge *Trinosophes*, of Paris: it was from Brussels that the first call had come; Paris answered, and following Paris, almost all the Masons of Europe gave money and took widespread action in favour of the Greeks; Masons took up arms and seventy brothers perished in Ipsara.

Almost all the glorious names of the revolutionary movements that led to the triumph of Italian unity were on the lists of Masonry; Giuseppe Mazzini and Giuseppe Garibaldi are worth mentioning.

Undoubtedly, even in Italy, from 1814 to 1860, Masonry was persecuted, but the lodges that managed to continue their work despite police surveillance and government inquisitorial measures, were all the more zealous and ardent.

Giuseppe Mazzini was praised by a Masonic writer. "He had, to the highest degree," he said, "that which honours the human species, absolute detachment, disdain for everything that was not his doctrine, his party, his faith. No one has more often than he braved exile, poverty, death and, what is worse, ingratitude and slander." Born in Genoa in 1808, Mazzini died in Rome on 10th March, 1872. On 15th March, the Grand Orient of Italy invited all Masons to gather on the following Sunday in the Piazza del Popolo in Rome to take part in the funeral ceremony; for the first time, the Masonic banner was displayed in the Eternal City.

Giuseppe Garibaldi, born in Nice in 1807, died in 1882 on the island of Caprera. He had been initiated, in 1844, in the lodge *The Asylum of Virtue*, in Montevideo, which was an irregular workshop. Soon after, regularisation was proposed and he was admitted to the French lodge of the same city, *Les amis de la patrie* [Friends of the Fatherland]. After the liberation of Sicily, several lodges in Palermo created a large independent lodge; Garibaldi was elected Grand Master. When, in 1895, the twenty-fifth anniversary of the fall of the popes' temporal power was celebrated, the Grand Orient of Italy addressed a circular to all the Masonic powers of the world, where it proudly proclaimed that Italian Masonry had worked for the unity of the fatherland and the destruction of theocratic government.

VI

As we have seen, Freemasonry need have no fear of judgement of its history. The heroic services rendered can be summarised thus.

In almost every country across the globe, for nearly two centuries it has been the educator of a great number of men from all classes of society.

An illustrious member of the brotherhood, Jules Ferry, described its work. When asked how Masonry constitutes a precious instrument of moral culture, he responds in these terms: "First of all, it is because it develops solidarity by practising solidarity; but above all else, another feature of the institution which is wholly fundamental is the spirit of equality which is the very essence of its doctrine and practice. Its greatest character, its social significance, is in this fact; the rich and the poor, the learned and the ignorant, are united in the same temple."

The Masonic scheme in religious matters has been applied as much in individuals' lives as in each State. Its very essence opposed the pretensions of priests of all denominations. The aim of Masonic doctrine was to fortify and consolidate the secular spirit. From there, to bring about the decline of fanaticism. People no longer lash out at one another because of their religion; civilised governments no longer persecute their subjects because of their beliefs. The influence of the lodges is so well demonstrated in this area, that precisely where they are forbidden, particularly in Russia under the Tsars, the abominable regime of persecution in religious matters continues to be rife.

By affirming freedom of choice, by recognising the fact that this is not only a right but also a duty, since only the free use of thought makes discovering the truth possible, Masonry leads to the study of all aspects of morality, philosophy, politics; it stimulates curiosity; it promotes experimentation; it is thus one of the chief causes of the speed of progress in the modern world, which contrasts so happily with the slow evolution of antiquity and the Middle Ages. As we have said, without the great number of converted men who have hurried and who are still hurrying into its temples, the causes of justice and tolerance would not have triumphed to the extent that they have. Masonry can be proud, more than any other institution in history, of having promoted the love and respect of the beneficent motto: Liberty, Equality, Fraternity.

www.ingramcontent.com/pod-product-compliance
Lightning Source LLC
LaVergne TN
LVHW101504200926
848483LV00001B/220
9781912142347